SUPER SELF
A Woman's Guide to Self-Management

SUPER SELF

A Woman's Guide to Self-Management

Dorothy Tennov

Funk & Wagnalls
New York

LIBRARY OF CONGRESS CATALOGING IN PUBLICATION DATA

Tennov, Dorothy.
  Super self.

  Bibliography: p.
  Includes index.
  1. Women.   2. Self-evaluation.   3. Success.
I. Title.
HQ1221.T27   158'.1   76-41721
ISBN 0-308-10273-8

1 2 3 4 5 6 7 8 9 10

For
my mother,
Lois Miller

Acknowledgments

I wish to express my gratitude to Lolly Hirsch, Helen Payne, and Vera Stecker for their reactions and support; to Frances Foster for her help with analysis of student self-management reports; and to Jonas Trinidad, Sharon Jordan, and Lisa Cook for assistance with various aspects of the preparation of the manuscript. Thanks also to Ray Hessels, Nelam Hill, John Jacobson, Tom Schmid, and Matt Vittucci, who read portions of the manuscript and by their reactions made me feel that this woman's guide to self-management has possible relevance to men.

Very special thanks to Finn Tschudi, for his detailed analysis and specific suggestions, and to Linda O'Brien, whose editing made this a much better book than it would ever have been without her.

And to my mother, Lois Miller; my aunts, Lucille Fuhrmann and Ann Nystrom; my grandmother, Rhoda Waldron; my brother, Daniel Tennow; and my sons, Daniel, Russell, and Randall, my gratitude for support and encouragement that was sometimes direct, sometimes very indirect, but always felt and always appreciated.

Contents

Why
Self-Manage?

This book will set you on a deliberate course of managing yourself for yourself. If you feel you are doing well now, you are ready to go on to becoming your super self. If you are not doing well now, the change may be even more dramatic. You will learn to actually do what you later will be glad you have done—and to do it in comfort, without the pain of gritted teeth and forced action. You become what you want to be by gradually stretching your inclinations and your capabilities until your actions are in perfect accord with your ambitions.

Self-management expands and increases your pleasures in life because the greatest joys are derived from accomplishment. (And the reverse is also true: Depression can result from knowing that long-range goals are going down the drain.) With self-management you will be able to look back on each day filled with the joy and self-satisfaction that come from knowing that your ultimate goals have come closer to your grasp.

Furthermore, the gains you make will last. A few days ago a friend telephoned in great excitement. "My whole life has changed. Now I realize that I was actually standing in my own way, that I was failing because I had not learned to think success," she said.

1

"Think success?"

"Well, I used to feel that my life just wasn't all it should be. But that was because I concentrated on what was going wrong instead of on what was going right. After all, it is how you think that determines how you feel. I've learned new thought patterns and I'm feeling great. I've come to accept things, not get upset over them."

It turned out that my friend had read a book about "thought changes." She really did seem to feel better than she ever had. Unfortunately, it didn't last.

Positive thinking may be powerful, but to be sustained it needs to be fed. I'd never knock it, but I would not rely on it. Not by itself.

Most of our feelings are reflections of the real events in the real world around us—primarily the words and actions of other people. If positive thinking causes us to engage in more positive action and if that in turn changes the actions of others toward us, then the happy results might well persist. But it is chancy. Self-management is not in conflict with positive thinking, but it emphasizes positive action, not just thought. It does not exhort you to appreciate yourself as you are and your life as it is. It means finding strategies through which your life will become what you want it to be to the limits of your inborn talents and within the reality of your external situation.

You may feel that you are limited by the demands of others—that the boss dictates, the baby dictates, the inevitability of the six o'clock dinner hour dictates—and that you are doing all you can already. You feel that the problem is not in you but in your situation. Of course there are and always will be limitations, but the limitations imposed by factors beyond your control are usually not the ones that really get you down.

But past performance is a very inaccurate measure of your true ability. Let's be nice to ourselves; risk belief in ourselves. The results of managing yourself will make you more interesting and many things in your life easier.

Many things are possible once you know how to use self-management. Most people begin by losing weight, exercising regularly, or putting an end to the tobacco habit. Then there are many other things to try. Do you want to work toward a promotion? Organize your housework? Go back to school? Start your own business? Learn to sew your own clothes? Become a gourmet cook? Deal with your children and husband more effectively? Have them treat you differently? Have a more satisfying sex life?

You begin a self-management program simply by watching yourself without trying to change anything. Just notice what you do. What time do you get up in the morning? Why at that time? What do you do first? Then what happens? Watch yourself through your day. Don't try to control anything; just observe.

Then you will analyze your schedules; you will examine your feelings as you progress through your days; you will examine what you do, both what you seem forced by external events to do and what you do when you are left to your own inclinations, free to do whatever you like. You will always begin with where you are.

Next you will, very gradually, through careful planning that ensures progress without pain, see what changes might possibly make for improvement. You will begin to keep certain records, which are useful in helping to plan the next step without going too fast. They are also extremely important in helping you to acknowledge some of the initial effects of your first efforts and in allowing you to enjoy the small successes along the way. They will reinforce all those intermediate steps and your progress toward your first primary goal.

Your life-style will gradually change. Your confidence and self-respect will grow. Soon you will be doing things you had completely given up on. With self-management, progress will be both gradual and inevitable.

You will manage your life to please yourself. You will develop a method that can be adapted to anything you choose. You will fill in your own details, your own goals, as they emerge. I will teach you how to set your course; you decide the compass points.

The workability of these techniques lies in their simplicity. This book is the key to their effectiveness. They are based partly on recent research by psychologists who used laboratory-tested techniques. They are also based on common sense.

Follow the plan, step by step. Gains may be slow at first, but success will ultimately and assuredly be yours.

This book is about how to do what you really want to do. Follow it, use it, and you will find yourself on the way to becoming your own SUPER SELF.

Analyzing Your Activities and Capabilities

Your Daily Schedule

Whether or not you have ever thought about it, we all have some kind of daily schedule which tends to repeat itself during the week and undergo certain changes on weekends. Much of it is imposed by outside commitments. But even if this were not the case, you would find yourself behaving in repeated patterns just because we are all creatures in whom biological and psychological rhythms occur. The biological functions such as urination, impulses to eat, and fatigue, as well as intellectual activities, tend to occur in daily, or circadian, cycles. Before attempting to introduce any changes in your situation, you must first get a good grasp of what that situation is. A good self-management plan—one that works and works comfortably—takes into account exactly where you are when you begin.

The Varying You

You are not always the same. Sometimes you are tired, sometimes you feel so good you could leap for sheer joy, sometimes you are lonely, sometimes you are overwhelmed. Scientists have just begun to discover some of the reasons we are as we are at different times of day and at different weeks of the month and even months of the year. There are regular cycles of virtually every body function, it seems, and all of these interact in complex ways. In each twenty-four-hour period, there are cycles of eating, sleeping, temperature, blood circulation, elimination, and of mental functions such as the ability to perform complex and repetitive tasks. Some of these appear to be related to known changes in the functioning of internal organs; the source of others is still not known.

If you think that your mood depends on the situation you are in and the things that you are doing, you are right, of course. Partly, it does. But aside from the gloom that descends when something goes wrong, or the joy you feel when you hear from an old friend, or the fatigue that results from overactivity, there is a fundamental rhythm that is characteristic of you, a waxing and waning of your energies and capabilities. For example, if you are a "morning" person, you will still be more capable in the morning, even on your worst days. If your most capable hours are in the early afternoon, even on your best days, the afternoon is likely to be the best time of day.

You may be unaware of the physiological bases of moods, inclinations, and capacities. But you will be able to assess them and to use your sensitivity to their changes and their regularities in the ordering of your days and your life. You already do much of this unconsciously, or out of plain common sense. What you will learn to do in this chapter is to refine your sensitivity so that you can make much better use of yourself as you undergo the changes that are constantly recurring. You will learn how to analyze the moments of your day and to analyze how you feel at various times of day. You will use the notion of "capability level" to determine when, how often, and under what circumstances you are doing things that are not really what you should be doing at that particular time. It can become a very easy and obvious strategy, as you will see.

Capabilities and Their Fluctuations

Begin by making a chart like the one on page 8. Notice that it contains two boxes for each hour of the seven days of the week. I began the day at 5:00 A.M. because few people begin their day earlier than that. (If you are one of those few, alter the list of hours of the day in the left-hand column accordingly.) Each hour of the day in the Capability Levels Chart has space for two numbers: the box on the left is labeled A for activity; the one on the right is labeled C for your feeling about your true capabilities at that moment.

The purpose of the Capability Levels Chart is to enable you to analyze your days to see how well your capabilities and the tasks that you engage in fit with one another. Since we know that we vary throughout the day, we want to determine how well what we do is related to our potential for accomplishment at each hour of the day.

Your Capability Levels

We distinguish five levels of capability—from most capable (Level One) to least capable (Level Five). What you can do at each level is an individual matter, and everyone varies. What one person can do at Level One may be what another can do at Level Two or even

Capability Levels

Hour	Monday		Tuesday		Wednesday		Thursday		Friday		Saturday		Sunday	
	A	C	A	C	A	C	A	C	A	C	A	C	A	C
5:00 A.M.														
6:00 A.M.														
7:00 A.M.														
8:00 A.M.														
9:00 A.M.														
10:00 A.M.														
11:00 A.M.														
NOON														
1:00 P.M.														
2:00 P.M.														
3:00 P.M.														
4:00 P.M.														
5:00 P.M.														
6:00 P.M.														
7:00 P.M.														
8:00 P.M.														
9:00 P.M.														
10:00 P.M.														
11:00 P.M.														
MIDNIGHT														
1:00 A.M.														
2:00 A.M.														
3:00 A.M.														
4:00 A.M.														

Chart 1. Under A, record the level required to perform the task you are engaged in efficiently and easily. Under C record the level you feel you are capable of reaching at the time.

Three, because what is easy for one person may be hard for another. Yet for each person the levels tend to occur more or less at the same time each day.

Level One. At Level One, you are at peak condition, capable of doing the best you can ever do. If you teach, this is when you can really get your points across. If you play tennis, this is when you are able to play your best strategic game. It is a time when you can take on problems that would be impossible for you to solve at other times. You may or may not be at your physical peak then, but you are at your creative, problem-solving peak. It is the best state to be in for planning, organizing, and making important decisions. It may or may not be you at your most joyous, but it is a you bursting with the feeling that you are able to take on the toughest jobs *you* will ever take on.

If you are puzzled by Level One, if you feel that you cannot remember *ever* feeling that way, you are not unusual. Many people do not realize what their capacities really are. They don't recognize Level One in themselves and don't utilize it. Instead of feeling on top of the world and ready to undertake decisions and activities that are the toughest you'll ever attempt, you may feel irritable at the time of day when you could be at your best.

Very often, when people begin tracking their levels, they find no Level One at all for weeks at a time. Later, even when they have learned to recognize and use their top level, there will be days during which it does not occur. These are days of illness or feeling down or of exceptional tiredness in which they will still not quite get up there. And sometimes we can find no reason why Level One does not occur on a particular day. We learn to wait until it comes again without feeling that we are at fault in any way.

Level Two.   This is a high level also, just under your peak. At Level Two, you can do many, but not all, of the most difficult things you will ever be able to do. Or, if you do these things, you won't do them quite as well or as brilliantly as you can at Level One. The important thing about Level Two is that it is not Level One. When you learn to distinguish between them, you will learn not to undertake things that are beyond your capacity even when you are at a fairly high level.

Level Three.   This is the middle level. Probably, it is the level at which you ordinarily carry out your most usual tasks. You can accomplish even fairly difficult tasks so long as they are already familiar to you. But you probably should stay away from major decisions and should not expect to be able to do the kinds of original or new things you can do at the higher levels.

Level Four.   Here you are definitely under par. Mentally, you want to take it easy. You don't want to try to learn anything, to read difficult material, or make decisions. Your focus is narrower; you can take pleasure in doing simple things, but anything more demanding than that is risky. You will see that Four is a very useful level provided your activities are fitted to it.

Level Five.   The only level lower than Five is sleep. At Level Five you can watch television for entertainment, take a shower, or carry on a conversation with a friend. But decision-making is hazardous and sustained concentration is absolutely impossible. Seldom does a really new thought occur to you at Level Five.

Now think about your own levels. What do you think you are capable of at Level One? What are your usual Level Four activities? It helps to make a list of various tasks and activities and, after each, write down the number that seems to fit each activity. For example, writing a business letter: How much capability does that require? More, maybe Level One or Two, if it is something you don't do very often, and maybe Three or even Four if you write many similar letters as part of your job. What about reading a story to your children? Where would you place that? For most of us, that could require more or less capability depending on how we go about it and, again, how frequently we do it. New tasks always require a higher level. It's hard to learn anything at Level Four and impossible at Level Five.

Your Activity Levels

The purpose of analyzing your day is to ultimately manage a good fit between your capabilities and the activities you undertake. An activity level is defined by the level needed to accomplish the particular task or activity comfortably and efficiently.

The activity level corresponds to the capability level that you need to perform a task with ease and yet just the right amount of challenge to keep it interesting. During a typical day you will go through all of your levels, even Level One, once you have become sensitive to it and learn how to use it.

If an activity is something you can do at Level Three, call it Activity Level Three. If you can do it best at Level One, rate it at Activity Level One. For example, suppose that at 10:00 A.M. on a Monday morning you are operating the switchboard at the office. You have previously decided that this is an activity which you can do efficiently at Capability Level Three. Mark a "3" on your chart under "A" for Activity at 10:00 A.M. Then try to evaluate your actual capability level at the time. Are you just a little bored or maybe just a little overwhelmed? If you find that you are edgy, if your thoughts are wandering to more complex things, maybe you will estimate your capability at that time as Level Two, or even Level One. If things feel right, if you are doing your job well and feeling neither bored nor overwhelmed, then you may estimate your capability at the same level as the activity, Three. On the other hand, if the task is difficult for you, if you are struggling to do it well because it seems a little too much for your capability level, then you will write down a "4" or even a "5" as your estimate of your actual capability level at the time. Write your estimates of actual capability, of the level of tasks you *could* perform efficiently, under C (for Capability) on the Levels Chart.

Warning: You can do simple tasks at higher capability levels; you cannot do, or can only do with much difficulty, error, and inefficiency, tasks that require a higher level of capability than you have at the time. In labeling your activities, assign the *lowest* capability level at which the task could easily be performed.

When you make up your list of activities, don't limit yourself to things you actually do. Also consider things that you would like to do but don't do, or haven't found the time or energy for in a long time. Successful self-management means doing what you want to do, not only what is immediately gratifying but also what you aspire to do. If you list these things at the outset, you will find it easier actually to fit them into a rearranged schedule later on. For example:

Martha wrote down "learn to crochet," and she estimated that it would be a Level Two, maybe even a Level One activity at first. Later, when she got better at it, she would probably not require such a high capability level.

Tasks that are at Level Four after you have learned them and become accustomed to doing them frequently may have required Level One to learn in the first place.

Recording Your Levels

After you have thought about your own capabilities at each of the five levels from One, when you are at your best, to Five, the lowest, you will start to collect data. Give yourself at least two weeks, longer if you feel you need it.

Carry an index card and pencil in your pocket, and for each hour of the day write the number that corresponds to your activity in the A column and the number that corresponds to your estimate of capability in the C Column. Sometimes this will be very easy to do; at other times you may be less certain. If deciding on the number is really hard, you can use fractions. If, for example, you think you might be at Level One, but you are not quite sure, though you know you are at a fairly high level, you could call it 1½. But it will be easier to get averages if you use whole numbers, so try, wherever possible, to do so, even when you are somewhat uncertain. Estimating capability levels is a subjective matter, but after you've been doing it for a while, you will begin to get a good sense of your own different levels. *Warning:* If you forget to record, just leave the space blank. It is very hard to estimate your capability level after the fact. If you have too many blanks, it will be hard to get reliable averages and you may have to continue a little longer, but that is safer than trying to judge how you felt an hour or more earlier in the day.

When you have finished collecting the data on which your levels analysis will be based, you will have two sets of numbers for each hour of the day—one for the levels required by your daily activities (A) and the other for your capability estimates (C).

Now get out your pencil and paper, and your calculator if you have one, to make things quicker, and add up all the numbers for each hour, then divide by the number of days (fourteen, if you recorded levels every day during the two-week period). When the results are plotted on a simple graph, you will get a picture of your fluctuating capabilities and of your periods of overemployment and underemployment.

Overemployment and Underemployment

We use the concepts of "overemployment" and "underemployment" to refer to poor fits between your capability and the tasks you perform. When you are overemployed, you are burdened with a task that is, at least for the moment, if not totally beyond you, at least difficult. When you are underemployed, you are engaging in an activity that does not make use of your current level of capability. The former is frustrating; the latter is wasteful.

When you are engaged in a task too demanding for you at the time (overemployed), the work will seem hard and you will really have to push yourself to get it done. This is not only inefficient because of errors you are likely to make, but it can also be very unpleasant. But the opposite, underemployment, is scarcely better. If what you are doing requires a Level Three and you are at Level One, it is wasteful and can be boring and frustrating. Of course, you can adapt somewhat to underemployment by creative imagination and rich fantasy, but most of us would rather use our higher levels for our more demanding tasks. We don't like to waste time.

So neither overemployment nor underemployment is desirable.

Jane Doe—A Sample Case

In order to give you a better idea of how the chart is prepared and how it is used, we can describe the case of "Jane Doe." Jane herself is a composite of several different people, but the experiences and details described are all parts of actual cases.

A graduate student in her mid-thirties, Jane is divorced and has three children—ages five, eight, and ten. She returned to school a year ago after six years of marriage. Her field is sociology, and she is in her second year of a doctoral program. She supplements the child support she receives from her ex-husband by typing for one of her male instructors and by tutoring three high school students in mathematics. She and her children live in a five-room apartment on the upper floor of a two-family house. They do all their own housework.

Before she began to try to keep track of her capability levels, Jane made a list of things that she felt she was able to do at each level. She included not only the type of activity that she was ordinarily required to do and ordinarily did actually do, but also things she would like to do if she could find the time. She spent several days listing her activities and trying to be very sensitive to how difficult or demanding each activity was so that she could give it the correct level number. She finally came up with the following breakdown.

Level One.   Write original draft of my term paper. Read scientific articles critically. Prepare for an exam by reorganizing the material and forming new concepts. Comprehension of good lectures is best done at this level, but if a lecture is slow and repetitive, it is very difficult to tolerate. I really need Level One for preparing my income tax return.

Level Two. There are many important things that I can do at this level. I can study, read *The New York Times* quickly and well, tutor mathematics, prepare for a tutoring session, write a letter to the children's father discussing the need for him to provide us with additional financial assistance, pay household bills.

Level Three. There is not much real schoolwork I can do at this level except for memorizing and rereading. I can tutor if I must, especially if it is material that I know well, but I am not as good at understanding my pupils' problems and questions as I am at Level Two. If I am at Level Three in class, I am more inclined to take notes than when I am at a higher level because it is harder, on the spot, to pick out the more important from the less inportant points that the instructor is making. This is a comfortable level for supervising the children in household tasks, talking with them about their problems and activities, preparing menus, making up my grocery list, figuring out a new arrangement for the furniture in the living room, organizing the children's playroom, and planning a party.

Level Four. When Level Four is not accompanied by illness or fatigue, it is perfect for most household tasks. I enjoy mending clothes, folding laundry, and even vacuuming the floors. Usually, I like to have music while I work. Or I might watch a television movie while I sew or iron. I like to read stories to the children and play games with them. Four is a comfortable level when little is demanded of me. I really like to talk to my friends on the phone, or have visitors, at Level Four.

Level Five. This is my "take-it-easy" level. I might read a magazine or watch television. I can also bathe and wash dishes or do hand laundry, but don't want the radio on unless I am doing almost nothing but listening. It is my one-thing-at-a-time level. Even dealing with the children is difficult at this level, but, fortunately, it usually occurs only after they are in bed for the night.

Jane spent two weeks assessing her capability levels. In Chart 2, shown here, are her levels for just one day— a fairly good day. She was at Level One for two hours in the morning, although the rest of the day was spent at lower levels. After lunch, she found herself very low on the capability scale. This was her midday slump. There was another slump around dinner time, but it was not nearly so bad.

But that was just one day. We can tell something from one day, but not much. The day might have been un-

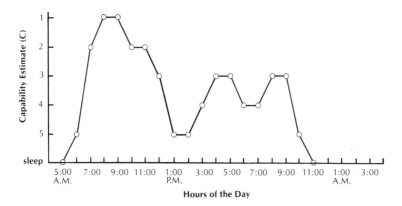

Chart 2.

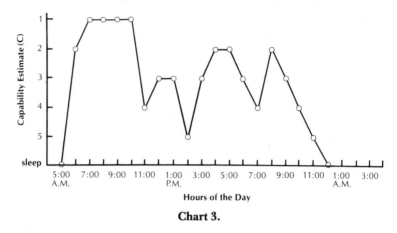

Chart 3.

usual and not at all representative. Chart 3 shows an even better day, in which there were four morning hours at Level One and higher levels in the afternoon as well. Once again, Jane attained her highest levels in the morning, followed by a midday drop and then another period of greater capability in the afternoon and early evening. Chart 4, however, is different. Jane described

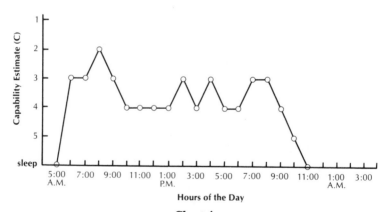

Chart 4.

it as "one of my worst days. I just never felt up to par the whole day except for just a little while at the very beginning of the day." Note that despite the overall low levels, the pattern of higher levels in the morning, midday decline, and higher levels again after supper was maintained.

Chart 5 presents Jane's average capability levels for the entire two-week period covered. Because the points in the graph are average points, the graph is smoother and the extremes are neither as high or as low as in the daily graphs. The average curve is affected by circumstances—especially those which occur at the same time each day—but it is better than a daily chart for getting an idea of the underlying levels because unusual circumstances that raise and lower levels tend to cancel each other out.

In Jane's average capability levels graph, we see two peaks. The first, the one that occurs soon after she gets up and lasts for about four hours, is the higher one. The second begins in the late afternoon and continues through the evening, but it is not as high as in the one in

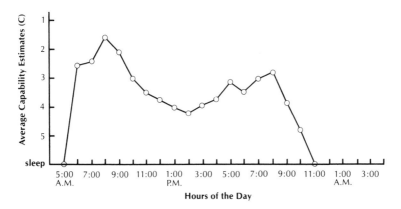

Chart 5.

the morning. The second slump around dinnertime that we saw in the earlier curves, is barely visible in the average curve. That's because it did not occur every day.

So far, we have looked only at Jane's capabilities as estimated by her feelings throughout the day. What about her activities? In Chart 6, Jane has plotted the activity levels of the activities in which she was engaged during one weekday. The first few hours were spent getting dressed, getting the children dressed, having breakfast, driving the children to school, and driving herself to the university for her morning classes. After class, she returned home to do household chores, pick up the children after school, go grocery shopping, prepare dinner, eat, and get the children ready for bed. Jane assigned all these activities to Capability Level Four. In the later evening, she met with one of her pupils, then turned to her own studying. It surprised Jane to find that so much of her day was spent engaged in activities that were relatively undemanding. She was especially disappointed in how little studying she was doing.

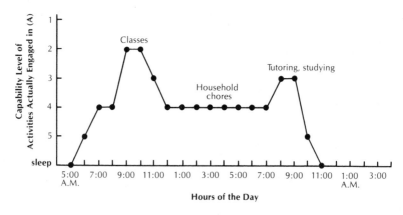

Chart 6.

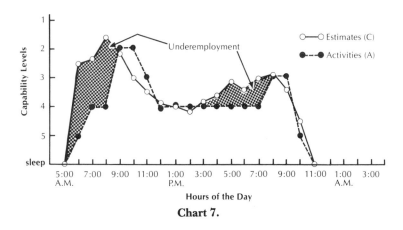

Chart 7.

Next, Jane plotted the average activity levels (A) and the average capability levels (C) on the same chart (7) so that they could be compared. She filled in the spaces in which capability level was higher than activity level, her times of underemployment. Jane was quite sure it would be underemployment, not overemployment, that would be her main problem, but the situation was even worse than she had imagined. There were seven hours of underemployment! No wonder she was so often frustrated and irritable, especially in the morning with the children, and in the evenings, as she nagged them to get themselves undressed and bathed while she washed the supper dishes and did other household chores.

The next question was what to do about it. After much deliberation, Jane decided on a radical but temporary step. Instead of getting up at her usual six o'clock, which is early enough for most people, she would change her sleeping schedule and get up at four o'clock in the morning! In this way, as you can see in Chart 8, she could study in the morning before the

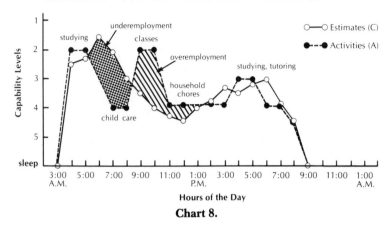

Chart 8.

children were up. Her classes, to which she had assigned the activity level Number Two, were now occurring at a lower capability level, giving her a period of overemployment, but this, she decided, was more tolerable than the wasted time of her present schedule. It meant taking more notes in class and sometimes using a tape recorder to which she could listen back in the evening or the next morning. She still had her morning high level while caring for the children, but it was less frustrating because she had already put in a couple of hours of work. The new schedule did not solve all problems, and it created some new ones, but it was an improvement over the previous one, and it was temporary—just until the end of the semester. She now enjoyed the afternoons after the children came home from school. On weekends the four of them would always do something: go to the zoo, visit their grandmother, go department-store shopping. At five o'clock, Judy, the high school girl next door, came over to give the children their supper and help them with homework and baths so that Jane could tutor and study.

The last chart (9) shows Jane's schedule for the following semester. Jane had returned to "normal" sleeping hours, and Judy came over in the morning to help the children get ready for school. Now Jane was able to work on her studies for four hours. Although she assigned Activity Level Number Two to these hours, in fact, she was often able to work at Level One during this period. Classes were reassigned to Level Three from Level Two. Now that she was preparing her work in advance, the lectures were easier to follow. When it seemed necessary, she would take notes or use her tape recorder. The midday and after-school hours remained the same except that now that they followed a good and productive morning work period, Jane found herself more relaxed and able to enjoy them. Judy now comes over in the evening after supper, at six o'clock instead of at five, to supervise the evening activities and to get the children ready for bed. But the children are becoming more and more accustomed to having their mother working hard at her studies and they are learning not to interrupt her and to do things for themselves. Jane can

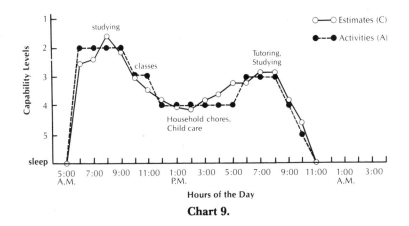

Chart 9.

anticipate that by the following year she will need less help.

In discussing the changes that rescheduling made in her life, Jane always emphasizes how much happier she is and how much happier, relaxed, and more pleasurable things are for the children as well. Although she spends somewhat less time caring for the children, the four of them spend more time having fun together.

"This is mostly," Jane said, "because I am no longer torn between wanting to be with the children and wanting to get my studies done. It was impossible to be relaxed when my work was falling more and more behind."

Examining Your Own Schedule in Terms of Levels

When you have collected records of your levels for two or three weeks, make up a chart like Jane Doe's on page 21 and plot the results so that you can determine your times of underemployment and of overemployment, if any.

Plot the weekends separately, and if any other day of the week differs regularly from the others, that day should also be plotted separately.

It has been found repeatedly that people on a self-imposed schedule tend to be underemployed. They often do not take on tasks that are as demanding as their capability level could accommodate. This is especially true of women who do not believe themselves capable of really difficult tasks. It is always possible to function at a level below one's current capability. How many women iron while at Level One, and what elaborate thoughts and fantasies do they entertain themselves with at those times! But, however easy it is to fall into, underemployment is ultimately wasteful and therefore frustrating.

When filling out your chart, be sure to evaluate your activity at the *lowest* level at which it could be done comfortably and efficiently. You will even find that some tasks are better—actually more accurately—performed at a lower level.

The case of Michele, a woman who took the self-management course, demonstrates why you should look at each activity very carefully.

Michele had assigned cooking Activity Level Two. "Cooking demands real creativity," she said, and I did not argue with her. But as time went on, she expressed increasing discouragement and frustration. The trouble was that the task of "cooking" needed further breakdown. Actually preparing a previously planned meal came closer to Level Four. But the planning itself, especially the way gourmet cook Michele did it, was definitely a Two for her. She rearranged her schedule so as to separate the two types of cooking activities. She planned at Level Two (in the early afternoon after her nap), and carried out her plans at a happy and unfrustrated Level Four in the evening.

Notice too what activities seem to require a higher level. It may just be that the activity had previously been scheduled during a period of overemployment. It seemed harder than it really was. The converse is also true. Activities which seemed easy because you had been doing them at a high level, when they *were* easy, might be given a number below their actual level. Don't be surprised if the level assigned to a particular activity must be changed a couple of times until you get it right.

Using the Capability Chart to Help Reduce Anxiety

We often expect too much of ourselves. At other times we expect too little. As soon as someone points it out to us, we are ready to agree that of course our physical fatigue, mood, and other aspects are continually changing throughout the day. And yet we treat ourselves as if we are to blame when we cannot perform.

The following two cases—that of Ruth and Claudia—reflect two contrasting approaches to carrying out school assignments.

Ruth's was a typical student pattern. Usually at the beginning of the semester, she would be given information from her instructors about whether there would be individual projects or term papers required for each course. The due date was also supplied in most cases. Perhaps because of past association with unpleasant circumstances, Ruth found the assignments anxiety-producing. She would take one look, say, "Well, it's not due for months," and put the assignment out of her mind. She might even lose the piece of paper the information was written on. Toward the end of the semester other students would mention term papers, thereby reminding Ruth that only a few weeks remained. But by this time, even if Ruth wanted to begin immediately, her other work had so piled up that she would have had to put it off.

Ruth is like the vast majority of students—she did her papers at the end of the semester, the day before they were due, usually at one sitting. What needless tortures such a method produces! The way anxiety functions in Ruth's case, as with so many students, is to make the working situation unpleasant. She did not begin until her anxiety over not getting the paper in was greater than her anxiety over working on the paper.

Claudia was a student who had taken a course in self-management the previous semester. When she got her assignments, Claudia analyzed each one in terms of its probable length, the amount of library work that would be needed, and how much time the actual writing would be likely to take. She also analyzed the task in terms of how much of her energies would probably be required at each level, and at which stages in the preparations of the assignments each level would be needed. Mostly the higher levels would be important during the organization and planning stages, when her creative powers would be most important. Claudia knew that her Levels One and Two, when they occurred at all during a given day, would always appear after she had been studying for about an hour. She made her plans for the semester as follows:

1. In order to be certain about meeting deadlines set by instructors and to avoid the end-of-the-semester pile-up, she set her own deadline for each paper one month before it was actually due. If her papers were finished, she would be able to devote all of her time at the end of the semester to preparing for examinations.

2. She ranked the papers from most difficult to least difficult in terms of originality and creative thinking needed. She planned that when she reached her high level, she would immediately begin work on the most difficult paper. When she had either come to a stumbling block, or had completed a certain portion of the first assignment, she would go on to the next one. The plan called for her to continue in this way until the more difficult planning stages for each of the papers was finished.

3. When the papers were planned and outlined, she would begin to use Level Three time for actually doing them. Since she had estimated their length, and had set a deadline date, she was able to divide the number of pages by days available to find out how much work would be necessary each day for her goal to be met. After she had begun the actual writing, she would end each daily session by counting the number of pages completed. This way she knew immediately whether she was ahead of or behind schedule. If ahead, she was delighted, and all the more free of anxiety. If she was behind, she knew she had to devote more time to the project in order to get back on schedule.

When you are aware that you have higher and lower levels of capability during the day, you no longer push yourself to do the impossible, or the very difficult. The pushing itself makes the whole task even more anxiety-producing. Claudia's comment at the end of the semester was that it had worked so well, "It felt almost like cheating. I got all A's for the first time, I had more time for leisure than ever before, and I could not believe how contented and happy I felt!"

Despite the inefficiency of the usual method, the one Ruth used, it is not hard to understand why she used it. We try to avoid that which is unpleasant. We literally forget. What most people fail to realize is that the same activity that is unpleasant and anxiety-producing when it is beyond our momentary capacity might be easy, even pleasant, if attempted when we are at a higher level. After you have begun to work *with* your levels, you will find yourself saying things like, "Sorry, this discussion is too high for me just now. Can we make an appointment to talk about it tomorrow or the next day?" And when you are not progressing well enough at some task, you will not say, "What is the matter with me? Why can't I do this? I guess I'm just too stupid to understand." You *will* say, "Well, I guess that's all for today. My Capability Level is not high enough just now. I'll try later, or tomorrow."

To get the most out of this form of coddling, to work at your level, and not allow yourself to be either overemployed (and frustrated and anxious) or underemployed (and bored and restless), you will plan ahead. Leave plenty of time for work at all levels. That's why Claudia set her own deadline well in advance of the one set for her by her instructor. "What if I get sick, or fall in love, or some other major distraction occurs?" she asked. "I'd be lost. I'd be forced to fall back on the old cramming method, and I don't ever want that pain again." Anxiety is so painful that planning to avoid it is really easing yourself into doing things that would make you very unhappy if they were left undone.

Hidden Levels

Some schedules are so contrary to what the individual's capacities are that the higher levels are masked entirely. The woman herself is unaware of them. This was the case with Marge.

Marge's alarm clock went off at seven forty-five. She dressed, had a light breakfast, and was on her way to work by eight-fifteen. The office day began at eight-thirty. Her secretarial duties began with mail-sorting and filing any papers or other materials left by her boss the preceding afternoon. Usually, she had just about finished these tasks when she was called to take dictation. In the afternoon, she typed and sometimes did research ordered by her boss in the company library.

Marge usually got home at about five-thirty. When she was not expecting guests, she ate a quick meal and then read the paper. Sometimes, when she was especially tired, she succumbed to television, maybe for the entire evening. "The only way," she said, "that I can avoid that for sure is not to start, not to turn the set on in the first place, which is what I manage to do most nights, but sometimes, I'm just too tired to resist."

When she could, Marge tried to work on her novel. She had outlined the plot and written two chapters two years ago, but the going had been painfully slow since then. Sometimes a sentence or two was all she could do. The lack of progress was depressing. In college, she had won several prizes for her writing, and the future had looked promising. Now she was beginning to lose all confidence in her ability.

When Marge filled out her chart, she made some important discoveries about herself. Like Jane Doe, she worked best about an hour after rising. Almost all work done on the novel since she had begun her secretarial job was done on Saturday or Sunday morning on those occasions when she did not have an overnight guest. During her Level One time, she customarily occupied herself with Level Four tasks—filing and mail-sorting! Among her office chores, these particular activities were relatively undemanding.

While she was uncertain about herself and her ability to write, Marge was understandably loath to make sacrifices in her social life. Now that she realized why she was having so much trouble, and that it did not mean that her ability had deserted her, she became enthusiastic about any change in schedule that would enable her to work on her novel during prime time. It turned out that the required change was rather drastic.

Marge changed her time of rising from bed to 4:45 A.M.—three hours earlier than she was used to. It took a couple of weeks to adjust, and longer than that for her friends to realize that she was serious about not staying up after nine o'clock in the evening. But the change ultimately transformed Marge from an anxious, chronically fatigued, nonproductive woman to what she had always wanted to be—a writer.

Before leaving for the office in the morning, she set her morning's work on top of the pile of papers that had become "the manuscript." In the evening, she read over the morning's work and made minor corrections.

Marge's friends learned that she was a good dinner companion, and that she could also be counted on for afternoons on the weekend. She began to take up golf and tennis—activities her guilt and depression had formerly kept her from.

Even Marge's boss was pleased. Now that her *real* work was behind her, Marge was a more relaxed and cheerful office worker, and since her chores were so easy for her, the quality of her work was maintained. In some areas, like filing, she actually improved because she did the work at a more appropriate level.

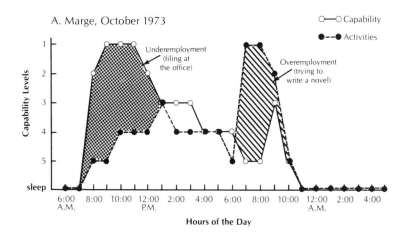

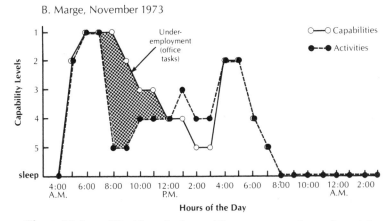

Charts 10 A. and B. Marge's charts. The upper one shows the original situation in which most of the day was spent either overemployed or underemployed. In the lower chart, the revised schedule shows more hours per day in which Capability level is matched with activity level. Some underemployment remains, and a lesser degree of overemployment.

Vicious Cycles

A vicious cycle is a series of events in which one event gives rise to a second which is even more negative than the first, and leads to a third which is still more undesirable, and on and on. Not working with your capability/activity chart can lead to the following type of vicious cycle:

Susan was worried about her sociology term paper. The very thought of it was upsetting. So she thought very little about it, especially when she was upset. A particularly unfortunate phenomenon was Susan's tendency when upset to choose an activity low on the scale. She would in fact be at Level One or Two when she began her work session, but the activity selected at that stage was a low one—Level Three, or even Four. Getting library books, perhaps, or looking up certain references. She was uncomfortable and mistook the discomfort for anxiety. Actually, it was boredom and frustration, combined with the tendency toward anxiety that is part of the higher levels.

It turns out that the same level at which we are able to be most creative and productive is the one during which our capacity for worry and anxiety is also greatest. Therefore, when Susan was at Level One, she was least likely to work on the sociology term paper. High-level "anxiety" acts as a spur to activity when one is truly functioning at that level. But when one is engaged in activities more appropriate to a lower level, the situation is annoying, and we are apt to be irritable. This, in turn, can cause other unfortunate consequences.

Dee's morning bad temper was something so inevitable that she and her family had grown almost accustomed to it. At least they had grown accustomed to avoiding her in the morning whenever possible. Her schedule analysis by her capability levels chart showed that she often had a two-hour period at Level One beginning about a half-hour after rising. When she gave up trying to do short-order breakfast cooking during that time and instead devoted herself to the much more demanding task of going over the books and making up purchasing orders for the family's small business, everyone profited. Including the business.

One of the most frustrating situations I can imagine is to spend capability levels One and Two doing activities at levels Four and Five, and then, just as the activity shifts to a more demanding one, have one's capability level sink. Yet this is the situation many millions of people are living with. Since they rarely if ever work at Level One tasks when they are at Level One capacity, they do not ever glimpse what their true potential is.

Shifting Too Far Downward

When we find that we cannot work at a given level, it is a common reaction for us to shift downward in activity. Instead, we should examine the first activity more closely, as Ginny did.

Ginny used to make all her own clothes at college and saved herself a lot of money that way. Now that she was working, however, she found it difficult. Her schedule analysis suggested that she did not divide the task of sewing into the activity levels it demands. She discovered that the task of making clothes consisted of almost all levels, from fitting and designing at the higher levels down to hemming, which she called a Level Five, suitable for doing with the television on. The hardest part of making clothes is the original fitting of the pattern to the person. To do the fitting after a day at the office just did not work. Now Ginny does the harder parts on weekends and the easy, relaxing parts during the week. She usually has several things she is working on at one time so that she can find something to work on whatever her level. If she cannot work at the level required for a particular garment, she shifts downward. She doesn't just give up altogether as she used to.

It is rare that a complex task does not involve several levels. This means that there are some aspects that can be tackled at one time and others that can best be taken on at another time. A very good example is an employment application form, something most people hate.

No matter what level you are at when you try to fill one out, it will be the wrong level for some aspects of it. If you are at Level Five, it will be easy enough to write in your name and address, but when you get to the part about previous employment and reasons for leaving, or when they ask for a brief autobiographical sketch, you will want to throw the whole thing away. If you are aware of your levels, you will save the hard part for when you will be functioning at a more appropriate level. Then you will be able to face the more complicated questions and those that call for originality.

It can be just as irritating to fill out the *whole* questionnaire while at a high level because using high-level time to write your name is wasteful and frustrating. The better you come to know your levels and what you can accomplish at them, the more acutely aware you become of the wastefulness of underemployment.

Lists can help you make better use of your levels. When something that must be done is placed on a list, the brain no longer need worry about that thing anymore; all you need do then is remember the list and check it over. Like Miriam, each person finds her own way to keep and use lists.

Miriam kept her lists in a single small notebook which she carried with her when she went out. At home, it could always be found in her handbag.

She had a list of heavy-housecleaning tasks that she would do when the opportunity presented itself, grocery lists for the various stores she shopped in, lists of books that she would look for during her next trip to the library, letters to write, phone calls to make, restaurants to try, and gifts to be purchased.

Every morning over coffee, she took about fifteen minutes to examine the various lists and to plan her day. She had found that the lists would only produce anxiety if she consulted them at a time when she was at a low level and unable to do much about organizing her time so that she could take care of some of the items. In the morning over coffee, her level was about Three and rising. It was an excellent time for planning.

Let me say it again: If activities are low level, it nevertheless often requires a higher capability level to plan than to carry them out.

Being Your Own Secretary and Servant

I'm sure we have all found ourselves wishing we had a servant or helper to do some of our lower-level chores for us. This feeling is particularly likely to occur when we are in the middle of one of our higher level—or at least average-level—tasks and we run up against a part of the task that is much easier than the rest.

For example, you have had a rather exciting time finding the references for your term paper. You have collected half a dozen books which contain very important statements. Now you must write down on your index cards: (1) a brief summary of the major points relevant to your paper, (2) any direct quotes you plan to use, and (3) citation information (author's full name, title of book, publisher, etc.). You have been working at about Level Two and that's where you still are. The filling out of index cards is drudgery. This is where you would like to delegate the task to an assistant hovering at your elbow, just waiting to take on low-level jobs when you are at a higher level.

Sometimes the best you can do with this situation is a compromise. You must fill out those cards; you cannot write the paper without that information. Depending on your situation (how easy it may be to return to the library and get the same books again, for example), you might adopt one of the following strategies:

1. Write down the author's name and the library reference number. Also write the summary, which probably requires a higher level and would be forgotten if you did not do it right away. Return to get the rest of the information later in the day or the next day.

2. Relax. Deliberately let your level slide down. Use the lower level work as a kind of rest. You might even find that you have some creative ideas while engaged in such tasks.

3. Combine the lower level task with something else that would bring it up to an acceptable level. Watching television or listening to the radio is ideal for this. Or you might have a conversation with a friend. In this particular situation, an earplug radio would be best. A conversation would not do, not only because of the need for quiet in the library but also because the task of copying information could be confused by the distractions of a conversation.

If you decide to do the task later, you have actually delegated it to your assistant—yourself at a lower level!

Formerly, when part of a housekeeper's task involved a lot of ironing, she would often divide the work into levels. There were the difficult things like frilly blouses and men's shirts. Such items required much more skill and energy than the easier items, such as handkerchiefs or pillowcases. Sometimes one of the children would be assigned the easy items; sometimes the housekeeper would assign the easy items to herself "later." She would begin by organizing the clothing and linens to be ironed, and she would do the more difficult items first. (This is one of our basic procedures, too.) By the time she got to them, her level had been lowered to theirs. In the same way, you can act as your own housekeeper—by doing your low-level housework at the right time for you. When you realize that organizing is itself a higher-level activity, you can become your own assistant. This is what happened to Lois.

Lois had analyzed her activity and capability levels, and her chart showed underemployment in the late afternoons. She also found that as she used her higher-level time more efficiently, her lower-level activities began to pile up. "I've become a good captain," she said, "but I need a crew!"

In fact, she had herself for several hours of the day at the right level for doing the neglected tasks. But at those times she as worker had no boss and was unable to know what needed to be done. The problem was easily solved. At the end of her higher-level work period, Lois learned to write out a list of things for herself to do as assistant. The tasks themselves were easy, but lower-level Lois would not have thought of them. Lois's assistant was herself.

When we begin to work at higher levels, our intermediate and lower-level tasks often suffer until we learn to incorporate them into our total schedule. One way to do this is shown by Wilma.

Wilma wrote out lists every day that would tell her what to do at each of her lower levels. As her day went on, she would decide on her capability level, then consult the list to see what chores were available at that level. Sometimes, reading the list informed her that her level was even lower than she thought and the originally selected lower level had to be revised downward.

When we make ourselves maximally efficient, we are as concerned about lower-level underemployment as we are about higher-level underemployment.

Living Life at All Levels

Too many of us go around feeling miserable because we have not found a way to accomplish the higher-level tasks. We knock ourselves out trying to do them at the wrong times and then feel even worse when we inevitably fail. Our anxiety goes up; our productivity goes down. We lose whatever self-confidence we may have had. It is no accident that we try to do high-level tasks at low-level times. Recall that at the higher levels, our capacity is greater for both work and anxiety. Putting off our high-level duties until deadline time is almost reached, we find that the anxiety level becomes intolerable just when we must work. At lower-functioning levels the anxiety is down and work is more tolerable.

This is often how potentially good students fail at their studies, as suggested earlier in this chapter. They meet deadlines by means of adrenalin (or amphetamines); they reduce anxiety (and level) by means of alcohol; when they finally do their work, they are functioning below their capabilities. They do not enjoy being at a high level because of the anxiety they experience at those times; they do not enjoy the lower levels because all they can think of is the neglected work. Often they attempt the task at lower levels only to fail and be further convinced that their ability level is low permanently, that whatever promise they may have shown earlier was some kind of mistake.

After schedule analysis and rearrangement, you will discover the joys that can be yours at *all* levels. There are few experiences more delicious than the guilt-free peacefulness of sitting on the beach at Level Four or Five, just listening to the crash of the surf and feeling the afternoon sun. There is a time for everything. The time for play is not the time for work.

But we must always start where we find ourselves. Examine your present daily schedules. Fill out your Capability Levels Chart and plot the results of a few days or weeks of daily recording so that you can determine where periods of overemployment and underemployment occur. Are there any changes in your schedule that could reduce them?

The following examples may give you some ideas.

Although she was very tired when she got home from work in the evening—Level Four or even Five—Vera found that a nap after supper was a good level-raiser. She also noted that very often the nap was prevented by telephone conversations. These were somewhat relaxing; they left her able to do light housework and watch TV. But they did not permit her to get any work done toward her long-range goal of writing and illustrating a book of stories for children. Only a nap raised her capability level high enough for that. The solution was to restrict use of the telephone. When she was ready to nap, she placed the telephone in the refrigerator, a very effective way to prevent herself from hearing its ringing. Under no conditions, she vowed, would that precious time be wasted.

With a similar problem, Mary found a slightly different solution. She used an automatic telephone answering device. When her work period was over, she listened to any messages that had been recorded and, if it was not too late, made the calls requested.

Rena had only one possible time in which she could work on her papers for school—while her two preschool children took their afternoon naps. She simply had to be able to work without interruption. The trouble was that she found herself too tired at those times. Too often, she slept while they did. Then she made a discovery. She was able to rest while they played in their playroom if she lay on the cot right beside them. Although the play was noisy, that did not bother her so long as they were not fighting over toys or getting into some kind of mischief. When problems arose, she found she was able to wake briefly and take care of them, then doze off again.

Lilian, with a problem like Rena's, hired a babysitter to care for her children while she rested and also while she worked on her school papers.

Because each person's situation is unique, it is impossible to provide specific procedures that will apply to all. Using the self-management principles as guidelines, you will be able to find those that work for you.

The Tactics
of Self-Management

Although this is a book about the management of behavior, I will talk more about what goes on in the head than what the arms and legs and fingers are doing. The brain is the control center for overt action. How the brain is organized, and what its orders are to the rest of the body, are what make us behave as we do. If we are "conditioned" to respond in a certain way to a particular situation, that does not mean that our arms and legs automatically act up as soon as we get near the controlling event. It means that perception of that event, or that stimulus, is likely to lead the brain to give out a certain order. Whether the expected (or "conditioned") response will occur will also depend upon what else is going on at the time in the brain. Self-management is a kind of behavior controlled by your brain.

Psychologists do not know nearly as much as people think they do. They have not even studied many of the problems that you would probably think they should have wasted no time getting busy on. But sometimes when researchers in their laboratories are studying something which would seem so remote and esoteric that no one could possibly imagine it having any usefulness, knowledge arises from that study that is really valuable on a very practical level. One such finding has to do with what is called the "channel capacity" of the human nervous system and the brain. It was found that human beings can only keep track of a few similar objects out of a larger collection of such objects at a time. A person can keep track of about seven similar things or ideas. The number may vary from about five to nine, depending on what is being dealt with and, maybe, on the particular brain. When forced to deal with more than that, the mind boggles a little. If we must take more than about seven things into account, some help is needed.

Now this magic "number-seven capacity" of the brain can help give you a basis for not taking on too much. It defines what too much is in quantitative terms. Too much is more than nine, maybe more than seven, maybe even more than five. On a practical level, it means that if you go to a party consisting entirely of strangers, you are likely to remember no more than about seven of them. If you are arranging a dinner party, you know that "intimacy" means keeping the number under nine, maybe even under seven, if you want each of the persons invited to be able to relate to each of the others. When I wrote my first book, I was afraid of getting lost if my outline became so full of topics that I could not remember the overall picture. By organizing the material into seven chapters, I never lost track of the major points I wanted to make. The magic number seven provides an example of how you can take into account what your brain is like.

Coddling Yourself

It is also an example of coddling. Coddling means not doing it the hard way; it means finding the way that is most effortless and realizing that the work should take place in the planning and in the head, not out there in the heat of the situation when plans have not been adequate. To coddle is to deal with the reality of the situation. In the previous chapter, we learned how to coddle ourselves by taking into account the reality of what we are like over the course of the day and trying to engage in activities suitable to our current capability. It is coddling yourself to avoid overemployment and underemployment. They are frustrating and inefficient. Coddling is not mere indulgence; it is a most essential aspect of self-management. Any previous attempts to improve your life may have failed because you pushed yourself unrealistically instead of coddling.

In this chapter, we will learn more tactics for coddling, that is, for successful self-management. I usually say that the first three rules of self-management are "coddle yourself," because, in truth, the other tactics are merely other ways of coddling.

The Principle of Taking Small Steps

Small steps means that we rejoice in a gain of small size; it also means that we set subgoals of even smaller size than our main goals. We know where we want to be at the end, and our goals are continually set closer to that final behavioral goal. But we learn to appreciate progress toward the goal. Small means enough to be accomplished. Sometimes, as the following example shows, small means remaining at the same level instead of backsliding.

Bea had been watching her weight by means of a graph. Her goal was to get her weight down to 115 pounds. It took eight long months to go from 135, her initial weight when the self-management weight program was begun, to 120, her present weight. She first reached 120 about three months ago. Not only has she not yet progressed further, but she has occasionally become heavier than that. Last month, she weighed 125 for almost a week.

Rather than being discouraged, Bea is glad to be able to maintain 120 until she can lose even more. A small step toward the final goal is to be able to maintain her present weight comfortably. She has already made significant progress in that direction.

Through self-management, you can create a new way of living for yourself. One of the most significant features of this new way is the ability to look further into the future in terms of goals and to recognize the part that the present plays in achieving those goals. When one small step is followed by another small step, progress is increasingly noticeable. A step which is of the right size should be large enough to be discernible, small enough to be accomplished. It would be wasteful to make the steps smaller than needed, of course. But because the goals of most self-management plans seem very far distant at the outset, the more common error is to make the steps too large in order to try to reach the goal sooner.

Baseline Measurement

A technique that helps us to decide just how large a step we should take next is that of "baseline measurement," or measuring one's behavior before a plan has truly begun. The term "baseline" refers to where you begin, to what the behavior is before any deliberate plan to change it has started. We begin any plan by measuring baseline. In the following case study, we see how even a serious situation must be approached first by baseline measurement.

Jody became interested in self-management largely because of her problem with schoolwork, which had become more and more difficult for her over the past few semesters. Unless change occurred she would be forced to quit. The instructor in her self-management class warned her that change would take time, that to rush would very likely mean failure, and Jody agreed to conduct the project as if the pressure were not extreme. In fact, she had been given a year to pull up her grades and show improvement.

The first thing Jody did was to observe all aspects of her studying and school-related behavior and to keep quantitative records of how much reading, homework preparation, and other school-related activities she did at home. Passive observation and data collection lasted two weeks. Since cutting classes had been a problem in the past, Jody also recorded classes attended.

She purchased a small notebook, which she kept with her at all times. Every time she studied, she wrote down the time she began, the time she stopped, the subject studied, and a letter grade from A to F, evaluating the quality of her studying. She also noted which classes she attended and gave separate letter grades for the instructor's "performance" and for hers as student. For example, if she asked what appeared to be a relevant question, she scored herself higher. If her attention wandered or she did not understand points made, she scored lower.

By the end of the second week, the following picture had emerged:

> *Studying:* Out of 42 sessions that took place during the baseline period, 20 consisted of reading English literature assignments, 10 were used for homework in mathematics, 6 for studying psychology, and the remainder were distributed over French and astronomy. The durations ranged from 10 to 36 minutes, with the following averages:
> English literature: 24 minutes
> Mathematics: 32 minutes
> French: 20 minutes
> Psychology: 12 minutes
> Astronomy: 22 minutes
> *Class attendance:* Jody attended all classes during the two-week baseline period.

Letter grades: Of the 30 class sessions attended, Jody gave herself A's once in psychology, once in astronomy, and four times in English literature. She gave herself an F once in math and once in astronomy. The rest of the sessions were mostly B's. It was in English literature that she scored highest.

The English instructor received almost all A's or B's; the math instructor received all B's; the astronomy instructor received one D, three C's, and two B's; the psychology and French instructors received all C's.

Jody felt that she was able to judge the instructors independently of her own performance except when she was in very bad shape (e.g., getting a letter grade of F herself).

Baseline recording has two major functions: It helps you decide on the size of your next step, and it provides a background against which your progress can be observed.

Subjective estimates without such measuring are often greatly in error. Suppose that instead of measuring her actual activity for a couple of weeks, Jody had merely estimated her performance. If she overestimated—if she believed that her average study session was two hours in length when it was really only a half-hour—she would probably set a goal for herself that would be too large, thereby violating the all-important principle of small steps. Underestimating, on the other hand, would be wasteful because it would lead to setting too low a goal.

It has been recommended that the first goal be set somewhere above baseline that would be a step just the right size. In the case of Jody's studying, this would mean somewhat longer than her average session of 22 minutes. A more complicated, perhaps better, plan would be to set different goals for the different subjects. Jody might, if she set out to improve her letter grades for class participation, set her goal for English higher than that, say, for French.

Define your progress in small steps using baseline data as a measure of initial level. The reason New Year's resolutions fail is that they usually consist of steps that are too large, based on mere subjective estimates of base line. (And, of course, the understandable but futile feeling that the goal must be attained immediately.) For a student who has been doing very little schoolwork to vow to get all A's during the next semester simply is not realistic. If the amount of work actually done were measured, a small-step interim goal could be set. It could then be accomplished because it would not be too large a jump from what had been happening.

The taking of baseline measurement should continue until you feel fairly confident that you have an accurate picture of the situation. You should adapt your recording to the specific conditions you are dealing with, as Helen was careful to do.

Helen recorded on a chart posted on her wall (1) the amount of time she spent watching television, (2) the time at which she began preparation of dinner in the evening, (3) how often she felt herself getting angry or annoyed at other persons in the household, and (4) the number of cigarettes she smoked. She hoped ultimately to watch television less or not at all, to eat at the same time every day, and to reduce instances of annoyance and anger, and of cigarette consumption. After two weeks, she found that television averaged 3.7 hours per day (a shocking figure to Helen), that dinner was begun as early as four o'clock per day, and that she smoked an average of fifteen cigarettes a day, less than she thought.

Because the average number of hours she watched television was 3.7, Helen felt comfortable about setting her first television goal at no more than three hours per day, at least for the first two weeks.

Cigarette smoking was also stable at between twelve and twenty. She set her goal at "fewer than fourteen."

She was less certain about the baseline data on getting angry. The recording period was unusual in that her two younger brothers were away. When they were home, it was most often at one of them that anger flared. Helen decided that she would continue her baseline recording for two weeks after her brothers returned in order to get a more accurate picture.

She decided to drop her plan to change the time of starting dinner preparation. During baseline, she noticed that other events, such as when members of the family came home, dictated the dinner time. She wished the dinner time were more regular, but to make it so would be very complicated because it involved other people and their schedules.

Some Effects of Baseline Recording on Behavior

Watching your own behavior, or anyone else's for that matter, is a very unusual activity. Probably you have never before done such a thing or even thought of doing it. People do not usually think of behavior in small bits, but rather in overall flows. They think of large units such as I-watched-television rather than I-watched-television-for-three-hours-and-ten-minutes. They think in units that seem meaningful to them. Were it not for baseline recording, you probably would not say *how long* you watched television, but what programs you saw. People are not used to observing specific actions nor to describing them quantitatively in precise numbers. This may be the reason for the strange and sometimes dramatic effects that baseline measuring can have in itself.

Sarah felt that one of her major hurdles in her weight-reduction plan was the way she filled herself with potato chips, candy bars, and other snacks that she obtained from the office canteen in the afternoon. She decided to baseline how many times she went out for a snack. She remembered that the day before she had made four such excursions, each time purchasing and consuming a relatively nonnutritious, fattening substance. Since she was sure of the number, she counted that as her first day of baseline. After that, for the entire two weeks of baseline recording, Sarah did not make a single trip to the canteen after lunch. She was surprised herself. She said, "I didn't mean to stop entirely, but knowing I was going to write it down had a definite effect. At first, I thought that I just wouldn't do it that day, then I found myself not wanting a snack. I think I'm cured, and I didn't even have anything to write down!"

Sarah also said that the day before baseline, when she went to the canteen four times, was unusual. A more accurate estimate of the number of trips she made was probably about four, or five a week, at the most. There was still a weight problem, but Sarah shifted her focus from office breaks to consumption of fattening foods at mealtimes.

Rita's venture into baseline measuring also taught her something she had not known before.

Rita wanted to get her little boy, four-year-old Hank, to be more helpful. She knew she could influence that behavior by rewarding small steps toward improvement. The problem was remembering to reward his behavior when it occurred. Often she failed to notice something he did that was helpful until too late. Rita knew that reward had to be contingent on specific behavior by Hank, not simply given out when she happened to think about it. The main problem was in getting herself to notice in the first place when Hank engaged in "good" behavior.

During the baseline phase, Rita kept index cards in the pocket of her jeans, and she spent a lot of time just watching her son and waiting for him to emit a behavior that she might reinforce. She was really surprised at the results.

"I had the image of Hank as a michievous child who was continually getting into trouble out of sheer boredom. Now I see that most of the time he is a model little boy, but I had been using his "good" periods to get my own work done and literally didn't see what a nice little boy I have."

There is much in our immediate environment to which we are totally blind. During the collection of baseline data, you will view the familiar in an unusual manner. Like Rita, you may be surprised at what you will see.

How to Keep Records of Behavior

Since how to keep baseline and other behavioral records is dependent on a great many aspects of each individual situation, the best I can probably do is to state what few principles appear to apply in most cases and give some examples. The first thing required is the ability to define behavior. Ask yourself specifically what it is you want to change. It took Chloe a while to do this.

Chloe wanted to have a "more sunny disposition." She decided that this meant that she would smile more often. She decided that during baseline she would note down every time she smiled. This did not work out so well, however, because she really was not interested in times when she would smile to herself or laugh at something she was reading, but only when smiles occurred in the presence of others. Accordingly, she changed tactics and tried to concentrate on smiling when others were around. Here, she encountered two additional difficulties: She would forget to notice when she smiled with some people, and she smiled a great deal, maybe even too much, at her twelve-year-old brother Mike and his antics.

So she changed tactics again and did not try to record smiles that occurred in Mike's presence. Also, it was not really the amount of smiling that was important, but whether or not she had in some way showed "cheerfulness" during social interactions.

So, after each social interaction, she tried to evaluate both how cheerful she felt and how well she had been able to express those feelings during the interaction with the other person.

Chloe found that redefinition of her behavior continued as her project progressed. But for now, we are mainly interested in how she kept her records.

At first, she used a small notebook. Each day, at the top of a new page, she wrote the date. Then every time she smiled, she looked at her watch or a clock and wrote down the time. Those records looked like this:

August 17th

9:00 A.M.	12:10	12:45	3:05	4:05
9:45	12:11	12:47	3:15	4:07
10:15	12:15	1:15	3:25	4:19
10:20	12:22	2:03	3:30	5:03
11:55	12:27	2:14	3:31	5:30
12:01 P.M.	12:33	2:37	3:34	5:45
12:03	12:39			

Then she decided that smiling to herself should not be recorded. At this stage, her notes looked like this:

August 19th

8:55 A.M.	11:50	12:22	12:50	2:10
9:15	12:01 P.M.	12:30	12:55	2:30
9:27	12:03	12:33	1:15	3:10
9:33	12:10	12:40	1:19	4:35
10:05	12:13	12:41	1:27	5:05
10:30	12:16	12:45	1:35	5:47
11:15	12:20			

The cluster of smiles around noon was because she had lunch with her brother; the absense of smiles during the afternoon was because she had forgotten to record. She was at work then, and busy, and she is certain that she smiled at some of the people she saw during that period.

During the final stage, she changed her method of

recording to this:

> August 24th
> 9:10–9:45   Ruth 3
> 10:14–10:33   Jim 2
> 11–11:05   Dr. Brown 4
> 1:15–1:25   Dr. Brown 4
> 2:05–2:15   Ms. Adams 2
> 2:47–2:49   Alec 1
> 3:15–3:20   Ruth 2
>
> Cheerfulness scale:
> 1. extremely cheerful
> 2. moderately cheerful
> 3. average or mildly cheerful
> 4. a little glum
> 5. very glum

Eventually, she decided that the problem of cheerfulness was very much limited to certain people—Dr. Brown, for example. It was because Dr. Brown provided very little reason to smile, and she realized that it was not mere smiling that would solve the problem.

In Chloe's case, the cheerfulness project did not go beyond baseline because what was learned during that period changed the way she saw the whole situation.

Ann also learned some things during baseline recording, but real progress began only after she adopted a better way of recording her behavior.

Ann's problem was her weight. I tried to convince her of the importance of regular, quantitative recording, but she was adamant: "I don't want to write down how much I weigh because it is too depressing; I really don't like to be reminded of it."

Instead, she decided to record what she ate each day or, rather, how often she ate. Her first records consisted of the date with tally marks after that indicated how many times she ate. At this stage she did not differentiate between eating a meal and eating a snack. If she ingested anything, she tallied it, whether it was a piece of candy or a steak dinner.

Ann's objective was to reduce the number of times per day that she ate anything. After a few days of recording, she found that she was eating less often. When she began baseline, she was eating about ten times a day. After a week of measurement the count had gone down to six, where it stayed.

At this point, Ann did not really have a specific dieting plan except to eat less. During baseline, a friend whom Ann had not seen for a long time and who had lost a great deal of weight came to visit. The friend advised that (1) Ann weigh herself several times a day if possible and at least upon rising and before showers, and that (2) the number of times of eating per day be *increased*, while trying to eliminate large meals and fattening foods. "Eating many times a day," Ann's friend said, "keeps you from ever being hungry, while avoiding eating a large amount at any one time, as one would do in a meal, helps keep the stomach 'shrunken.'"

Despite her earlier resistance to frequent weighings, Ann decided to adopt this plan. It sounded relatively painless, and her friend's lovely new figure seemed sufficient testimony to its effectiveness.

Six months later Ann had lost fifteen pounds. She said, "You were right about keeping records. The daily weighings really kept me in line. Although there were long periods of no change, I think I would probably have backslided if I had not kept those records all that time. In the end, they kept my spirits up because I could look at where I was compared with where I had been and see I was at least holding the line when I was not actually losing."

Sometimes collecting data, on index cards for example, is the first step in keeping your record, and charting what you have collected is the second. Because one's weight comes in a convenient numerical package (e.g., 135 pounds), there is only one step required—the second one. If you were charting the number of cigarettes smoked, or the number of times a day that you remembered to reward your child's good behavior, or how long you spent studying, you would first determine the day's results by writing the figures on index cards or in your notebook; then, each day, you would make a mark on the chart to show the amount for that day. In other words, for each day you plot how many or how much of something for your record. In a weight chart you read the figure directly from the dial on the scale with no need for further recording that day. Charting baseline and measuring the continued results of your self-management project is usually done in the same way. You use the same chart, but you continue to see whether changes occur. Keeping behavioral records may be an unusual activity for you, but you will find that in a short period of time it won't require much effort.

The following accounts of Ann's and Theresa's projects illustrate some more ways of keeping records.

Ann's Weight Chart

Changes in weight, especially changes that last, are likely to be the result of a long sustained effort. It took Ann six months to go from over 130 to her goal of 115 pounds, as is shown in the graph on pages 56–57. In fact, in the last graph, for September, we see that she has reached her goal on a couple of days but still has to work in order to stabilize and maintain it. Greatest weight losses occurred in April, the month she began her self-management program, and in August and September. In May, there were no gains at all, except that she managed to hold the weight loss she had already achieved. June and July showed progress, but very little.

Weight loss is one of those goals that must be thought of as taking long periods of time, a year at least—more than that for an extremely obese person. The charts, kept daily, provide information that can be related to current eating practices. The problem with the month of May, in Ann's case, was that the new policy at the office required employees either to eat at the company restaurant or to bring food from home. Ann ate at the restaurant in May, then began to bring less fattening foods from home in June.

THERESA'S EXERCISING PROGRAM

Finding she was successful at losing weight, Theresa felt it was important that at the same time she begin an exercising program that would help maintain her weight and would improve her health and appearance. To avoid taking too large a step, she decided she would begin with an initial goal of five minutes a day, before her morning shower. She set her alarm for five minutes earlier than usual and placed a chart on the wall on which to mark her morning's exercising time.

Theresa's graph for exercising is shown on page 58. Days of the week are marked on the horizontal axis, and number of minutes spent exercising on the vertical axis. Since she had not previously exercised at all, there was no need for a baseline. The horizontal lines at fifteen and at thirty minutes show Theresa's major interim goal and her final goal; these made it easier for her to see how close she was getting to her goals of extending the exercise period as she went along. As you can see from the graph, it took her about four weeks to reach her final goal.

Planning

Another concept and practice that is very important in self-management is that of planning. The reason

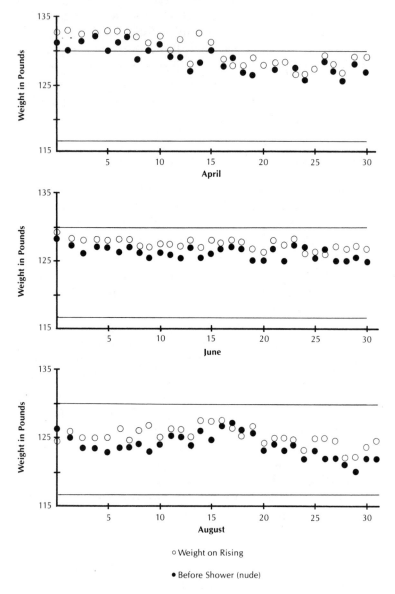

○ Weight on Rising

● Before Shower (nude)

Chart 11. Ann's weight chart.

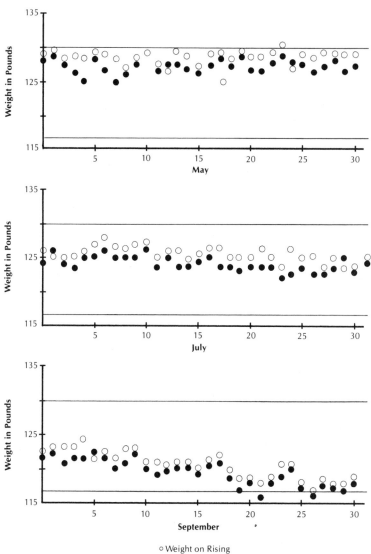

○ Weight on Rising

● Before Shower (nude)

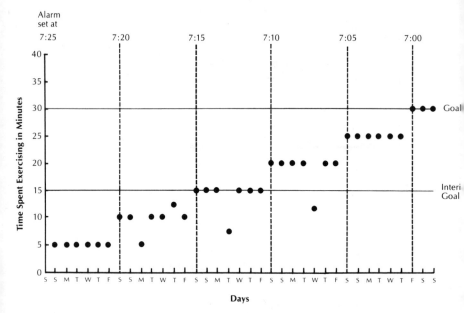

Chart 12. Theresa's exercising program.

home may trap you is that you are too likely to be unplanned there. We often fall victim to momentary impulses which tend to have only short-run consequences,
and forget entirely about things we really need to do to
protect our longer-range goals.

Planning to do something makes things easier in
many, many ways. We seldom think of everything at
once; planning ahead for something gives us time to
think through just how things may work out, what pre-
cautions must be taken, and what complications might
occur. Planning also helps in ways that are not exactly
deliberate and conscious. Your body and your mentality
has time to get ready; something sprung on you suddenly may be doomed to failure when the same thing
might have worked if there had been some preparation

for it. Knowing that a change will take place almost automatically leads to actions that will make the accomplishment of the change easier to manage.

You will see the importance of setting dates for beginning certain types of behavior-change projects and for many other things. While it is true that the flexibly scheduled vacation has clear advantages over arbitrarily deciding months ahead what city you will be in on a certain date, the former vacation must be more carefully planned in many ways than the latter. And the same kind of contingency planning, with built-in capacity to change as the situation changes, that is needed for your flexible vacation characterizes most self-management plans.

Among other things, planning can help you to remember to do things. Just as grocery lists help prevent unnecessary trips to the store for forgotten items, behavior lists can keep you from not doing something you wanted to do because it slipped your mind to do it. Grocery lists are common. Making lists of things to do before going on vacation is also common. Self-managers make those lists and many others as well.

Here's Cynthia's list for Saturday morning.

> Children to watch Channel Three at 11:00 A.M.
> Call Mr. Broome about fixing the back fence
> No other phone calls!!
> Gather outgrown clothing for the church sale
> Ask Tim nicely if he hasn't mowed the lawn by noon
> If Bunny calls, say I can't stop now but will call back later in the afternoon
> Take turkey out of the freezer
> Clean the bathroom

In her list, Cynthia anticipated things that she might

forget to do and things that she'd really rather not do—for example, talk on the phone to Bunny too early in the day or nag Tim about the lawn unnecessarily.

Such planning can really make life easier. It helps you do what you want to have done instead of what occurs to you to do at the moment.

Plans also help you to anticipate and to minimize problems that might otherwise have been serious.

When Judith thought about it that morning, she realized that there would not be time to prepare the dinner she had originally planned. She altered the menu to include things she could pre-pare ahead of time and store in the freezer. While she was at it, she also planned a short nap so that she would not be fatigued during the evening.

Before starting out for the park, Lily packed a lunch for herself and a bag containing Mary's bottle, diapers, and a change of clothing. She telephoned for the weather report and decided to add sweaters for both herself and the baby.

Before she went into the room in which her job interview would take place, Lee studied her list. It contained the following re-minders:

> Sit up straight
> Smile, but not inappropriately
> Speak clearly and audibly
> Feel proud, not apologetic, when telling of your previous
>   experience
> Answer questions directly; do not stray from the point

To some of you, such planning is obvious and habitual. But to others, it is not. In this book, you will find examples of planning in ways that you probably haven't thought of but that you will find can make life go much more smoothly. But remember, planning should always be a help, never a hindrance. As impor-tant as planning is, there should be room for changing

plans when the situation calls for it and when the unanticipated occurs. Too rigid planning can be even worse
than too little planning. The plan should not be thought
of as a blueprint to be followed precisely, but as a way of
reminding yourself to do things you might otherwise
have overlooked and a way of giving your brain plenty
of time to prepare for upcoming events. If your plans
are good, you will be able to deal better with surprises
than if you had made no plans at all.

The Principle of Reinforcement

Suppose you have several tasks ahead of you. If you
wonder whether there is any way of selecting the order
in which they should be tackled, the answer is: absolutely. All other things being equal, "work" precedes
"play," and higher-level tasks precede lower-level ones.

If you are a person whose daily high level comes early
in the day, this sequence is natural to you. But if you feel
that you can only reach high feeling levels late in your
day, sequencing can be more of a problem.

Even within a level, tasks should be arranged in a
hard-to-easy order. The more efficient students complete their mathematics assignment—if they find that
the most difficult—before reading their literature assignment. The housecleaner scrubs the floors before arranging the flowers. The musician plays scales before
working on musical selections, and she works on difficult passages in a new piece before rehearsing those
with which she is more familiar. The grade-school
teacher schedules arithmetic before nature study. Most
people eat dessert *after* their meal.

Occasionally, there are tasks that necessitate reversing
the order. In some exercising, one must do some easy
warm-up movements before the difficult ones can be
attempted. But even in such sequences, the last items

should be pleasurable as compared to others in the list.

Most current writers on self-management consider arranging hard-to-easy sequences an example of the use of the principle of positive reinforcement. This principle states that pleasant events strengthen the tendency to repeat whatever you were doing just before the event. If something you do pays off for you, you are likely to repeat it next time you get into the situation in which it occurred. The order in which behavioral events takes place is a very important aspect of self-management. The activity that follows the one you wish to strengthen is more effective as a reinforcer when it is a usual and regular activity. And, as the following examples show, it doesn't have to be highly pleasurable.

Martha spent a lot of time reading. She read two or more novels each week. What she had not been able to get herself to do was to study French vocabulary and write letters home. She worked out a self-management plan to improve the situation. Every time she picked up her book to read, she decided that she would let it remind her of the two behaviors that she wanted to strengthen. If she had written a letter within the last three days, she was okay; otherwise, she would write a letter—however brief, even if just a short note—before reading. Also, she kept her French vocabulary words near the book. Before reading, after an interruption of any kind, she would run through five vocabulary words. These were on cards, with the French on one side and the English on the other.

Linda noticed that one of her most regular activities was taking a shower in the morning. She decided not to "waste" it. She elected to put some household chore ahead of it. She made a list of suitable chores—they had to be "dirty" and also to be accomplished in a few minutes. If they took too long to carry out, she knew the scheme would not work because she would be late getting to the office. Her list included washing around the toilet bowl, taking the garbage out, shaking out the dog's bed, sweeping the front steps, dusting in the living room, and other items. At first, she could think of only a few things, but as time went on she thought of more and more suitable activities. She kept the list on the bathroom door, and before her shower each morning she did one of the things on the list.

The plan worked very well. Linda said, "I found the shower more pleasurable because I felt that much more in need of one. Even more important to me is the fact that those nasty little chores that I always hated—partly because they *are* dirty and I would already have showered when I thought of them—now those things are all done all the time!"

Parents find that getting children to clean up before meals is much easier when it can be made part of a sequence of things, provided the atmosphere of the whole project is a positive one. They do not make a threat out of it; they do not say, "There will be no meal (or reading or shower) until the toys are put away (or letter written or "dirty" task performed)." That would make it a situation containing an element of punishment. In self-management, we avoid the use of such punitive controls.

Putting a new activity before one that is already part of your schedule works well. The reason for this is not entirely known, but we know that it is effective. Martha was reminded to study her French by a bookmark that read "Study French Before Me," and the effort required was so small that it was silly not to do it. Also, it made the reading delightfully guilt-free. (That is my favorite explanation of why the scheme works.)

Often, we try to use the opposite sequence. We say, "I'll just read for a while and then I'll study." Or, "As soon as this television program is over, I'll get to work." Or, "You can go out to play now if you promise that you'll come in to do your homework when I call." It's true that nature does not always cooperate with our sequencing needs. The parent is in a true dilemma when doing homework first would mean missing the afternoon sunlight. In such cases, it is necessary to use something else as the follow-up activity in the sequence. Homework can precede supper in the chain of activities. And helping with after-supper clean-up chores can precede watching television. The activities then remain in the new-old sequence (or, behavior-to-be-strengthened preceding behavior-already-having-high-strength sequence).

Antecedents

We call any object or event that is often followed by a particular behavior the "antecedent" of that behavior. The presence of the antecedent does not ensure that an action will take place, but it makes it a lot more likely. For example, the fact that it is six o'clock and your dinner is waiting for you on the table makes for strong antecedents to eating. But if you have to make an important telephone call at that time, you will probably take care of the call first and then go to the table. The ringing of the telephone is a very powerful antecedent, or cue, for the behavior of answering the phone. Have you ever noticed how you feel an impulse toward that behavior even when it is someone else's phone that is ringing? Even when you hear a phone on a television show, you might detect a small impulse in yourself. This is an excellent example of an antecedent to a particular action, an antecedent that is usually obeyed.

When you begin your attempts at self-management, during the period of time you spend observing yourself and analyzing what you are doing, note antecedents wherever you can find them. Ask what cue precedes an action and seems to call it forth. Quite a lot of effective self-management consists in reminding oneself to do things through planting cues in the physical environment or in removing those cues that are associated with undesirable behavior, as in the following example.

Millie discovered that some of her overeating was stimulated by the candy and nuts which she ordinarily kept out in the living room "for guests." Millie found that most of her guests were also on diets and actually preferred not having such things around. Millie realized that she herself had been the one who ate most of it.

Removing antecedents that lead to undesirable actions is important in the early days of attempting a major change, especially with what psychologists call "consummatory" behaviors. These are things like eating, smoking cigarettes, taking "abused" drugs, nail biting, or anything else that produces its own reward. Such behavior is often connected to antecedents, or specific cues, as in Millie's case. In reducing the frequency with which you engage in such actions, look for things to do that keep you from thinking about or from wanting the substance you have decided to reduce or eliminate. This is another form of coddling. While the antecedents that lead to undesired actions are removed as part of a self-management program, others that lead to behavior you want to substitute for the undesirable behaviors are added. (For more about this, see "Consummatory Behaviors," p. 84.)

Rescheduling

One of the most useful self-management strategies of all is the rescheduling of ordinary events so that something for which you have very strong tendencies comes after something you are trying to build up. Often, we find it easiest simply to place the action we are strengthening right before a habitual action. Lilly's exercise plan involved both rescheduling and planting cues (antecedents) that would remind her to carry out her plans.

Lilly was prescribed remedial exercises and told by her doctor that they should be done twice a day without fail. The trouble was that Lilly forgot about them at the "right" times, then remembered them when it was very difficult to do them, at mealtime or after she was in the shower or in bed. She needed effective antecedents to exercising.

After reviewing her daily routine, Lilly decided that before breakfast and before her evening bath were the best times. The problem now was to find a way to remind herself to do it. She made two cardboard signs which read "Exercise Now!" One of them was hung over the shower, the other placed on the dining room table. They were designed to serve as belated antecedents if she had not already exercised prior to getting ready to shower or eat. Lilly also kept a chart on which she indicated how many exercises she completed each day. During the first week, she was reminded by the signs almost every time, but after a while the impulse to go to breakfast or to take her shower was sufficient to remind her to exercise, and the signs were no longer used.

This kind of rescheduling is very effective. Not only does the impulse toward the usual behavior remind us to engage in the weaker behavior—e.g., exercising, in Lilly's case—but there is greater pleasure in the behavior that follows. When Lilly used to sit down to breakfast and then in the middle of eating remember that she should have exercised first, it was rather unpleasant. Those exercises were very important to her well-being. To eat *after* exercising was pleasurable because of the satisfaction that came from knowing that the exercising had already been done.

You should always be watchful for the opportunity to reschedule, with the aim in mind of suiting the capability level to the activity level.

Geri was concerned about her French examination. She knew that cramming would never work, that she had to establish a regular daily practice of studying or she was lost. She estimated the task at about Level Four, sometimes Level Three, and she did not want to waste her Level-One and -Two time with it. Those levels were needed for physics and mathematics, which were much more demanding. Still, the French was essential. She could not afford to do badly in it.

She had scheduled her main study period for right after breakfast. She would begin by looking over her notes and writing in her journal, since it usually took a half-hour or so for her to get up to the necessary level. She decided that instead she would study French at those times, as a warm-up activity prior to her more difficult subjects.

It worked very well. That half-hour each day was enough to bring her mastery of French up to the level needed. She wrote in her journal in the evening, which actually turned out to be a better time for that, too. But what was most pleasing to her was the increased pleasure she derived both from the French and from the physics and math. Without her realizing it, the difficulty with French had been affecting her other work.

Susan rescheduled her mending of the children's clothing. Now she kept her sewing basket by the television set and mended as she watched the evening news, when she was at Level Five. Had the basket been upstairs in the closet where it was formerly kept, she would not have "had energy enough" to go up to get it. Since the change, not only does the presence of the basket remind her to sew, but she also places items in the basket carefully, with what is needed most on top of the pile.

Peg liked to make phone calls although they disturbed the momentum of the day. She also tended to talk longer than she wished when she did make them.

Most of her calls required only Level Four or Five, so the

phoning session was rescheduled to take place after her more demanding tasks.

She kept her running phone list on the table beside the telephone, and as soon as she had finished her more demanding household tasks, she sat down and ran through the entire list.

It has been said that the ABC's of behavioral change are antecedent, behavior, and consequence. The kind of behavior that we deal with mostly in this book is behavior that has repeatedly been shown to be affected by its consequences. If the consequences are pleasant, the act is likely to be repeated. This is the principle of reinforcement which I have already talked about.

When dealing with yourself, try to set up situations in which the consequences of the activities you are strengthening will have reinforcing effects. When you reschedule so that activities in which you customarily engage are preceded by the new acts you are building, the customary activities are more pleasurable because of the knowledge that the other behavior has occurred.

When you examine your daily schedule, you will probably notice that much behavior occurs in chains. For example, you usually wash your hands before eating. Being about to eat has become a cue for washing. As a child, you probably sat down to the table before you remembered to wash (or, more likely, we were given a parental reminder.) As an adult, you find it part of a behavior chain. You enjoy the meal more when your hands are clean, if for no other reason than that the dirtiness of your hands would otherwise continually remind you of something left undone. Washing before meals has become a "habit."

But habits, strong as they may sometimes seem, are never automatic; they can be changed. Suppose, for example, the water became contaminated and could not be used and it became undesirable to wash before meals. After many years of practicing one procedure, the new one could be learned in fairly short order. It would then be a good idea to place a cue in the form of a sign that said "Contaminated Water, Do Not Use" near the faucet. The impulse would remain for some time, or maybe a substitute for normal washing would be found. But changing that "ingrained" and normally desirable behavior would be possible; it would require only a procedure.

The same is true of any new behavior we want to make part of our normal routine; it can be done. When we find ourselves doing what we would rather not have done, or failing to do what we wish we had done, we must find a way to get around our impulses and inclinations. Well, that is what self-management is all about. Human behavior is very flexible.

New Behavior

Throughout most of this book I will talk as if you know just how you want to change. But deciding on what changes to make will continue to be a major problem for you—maybe even the most difficult problem of all. It is much easier to set goals about obvious things like weight, smoking, and studying-time. As important as those are, they hardly scratch the surface of what might be done to create the new, self-designed you. But your brain has been set along certain grooves, and it takes some strategies to shake it into new conceptions.

A very good way to find behaviors to change is to observe the behavior of others. Use others as models for your own actions, especially others who seem to be attaining the goals that you would like to attain for yourself. Watch them carefully. Note the details of their behavior. You might even question them about their daily routines. People generally like to tell others about how they achieved their goals. It is a matter of pride to discuss accomplishments. That is how Ginny got help.

Ginny knew that she was not very successful as a casual conversationalist. She had always assumed that her difficulties in that area were related to her general superiority in intelligence. Topics that were not "intellectual" could not sustain her interest for very long. But her appointment to an important office in college administration changed her feelings about the matter. She would never succeed at her job if she were unable to engage in ordinary chatter and small talk.

Martha, an acquaintance of Ginny's from college, was selected as a model because she seemed to be a very accessible person as well as the kind of conversationalist able to conjure up an interest in any subject. Martha used her excellent social skills in her job as director of sales personnel.

Ginny was frank about what she wanted, which was easy because Martha's apparent interest encouraged openness. She told Martha that she had always admired the way she put people at ease and listened to them with such obvious enjoyment. She asked if she could accompany Martha in some social situations in order to watch just how she did it.

The stratagems which Martha used were amazingly easy to detect once Ginny concentrated on exactly what Martha did in social situations. She looked directly at the person she was with, she called them by name. She gave periodic signs that she followed what they were saying. To Ginny's surprise, Martha said very little herself.

Watching and talking to others is probably the best way to develop new behaviors. Reading is another important way. Go to the library. Somewhere on those shelves are books on all types of self-improvement subjects. They are not all located in one place. In one section you will find books on dieting and nutrition; books on child care are elsewhere. Librarians are also great sources of assistance.

The most important thing is that you do not limit your goals only to those things you can think of at first. Hang loose. Be receptive to ways of behaving you might previously have found inconceivable for you.

Try always to remember that your feeble brain with its fixed grooves is self-management's worst enemy. Feed new information into it through active searching for ideas. The you you are at this moment is a joint product of your heredity and your environment thus far. Let this book be a new and important environmental influence, powerful enough to turn around some of the previous influences that have left you somewhat less than you want to be, and than you can be.

Shaping

"Shaping" refers to the strengthening of behaviors which are not your final goal, but which are definite steps in the development toward that goal. It is a continual process of interim goal-setting. Essentially, it is what we do when we measure baseline, then set our first goal just above baseline in a small step. When that step has been accomplished, a slightly higher goal is set, and so forth.

This process is easy to understand if you state your goals in terms of quantity—amounts to be increased or decreased—such as when you are trying to increase study time, or decrease telephone conversations, or take off weight. Sometimes, as we have seen, we want to shape entirely new behaviors. In other cases, it is improved quality of the performance of an old behavior with which we are concerned.

Linda set as her goal the learning of a Bach fugue on the piano. The ultimate goal was a perfect performance at the correct tempo. The first goal was to read through the piece by sight until it had become familiar to her. Then she worked on mastery of the more difficult passages. After that, she worked simultaneously on memorization and on interpretation.

Shaping is also very useful when we are trying to influence the behavior of another person.

Marcia wanted her daughter, Lindy, to learn "good table manners," and she had very specific ideas about what that meant. But Lindy, two years old, was a long way from where Marcia wanted her to be. The first interim goal was set at keeping the food on the high-chair tray rather than letting it get pushed to the floor. Whenever Lindy pushed food toward the center of the tray or picked up something she might have knocked off, she was praised. Later, the goal was keeping the food in the bowl and, still later, eating with a spoon, not spilling food from the spoon, and, eventually, eating with a fork.

So we coddle others as well as ourselves when we try to manage behavior. We use small steps that ensure success; we do not ask for that which would be frustratingly difficult and risk creating distress.

The Physical Environment

The home can be a particularly difficult place in which to change behavior because it contains many cues to the old behavior—antecedents that call forth actions that are just the opposite of those we want. The easy chair invites sitting, the television set is there to be viewed, the refrigerator can be opened for a snack, and the telephone brings forth images of the various friends we might call. Often we drift along, letting ourselves be attracted by the features of our environment in accidental, unplanned ways. We see the phone and make a call; we go to the refrigerator during TV commercial breaks; we plop ourselves down on the bed; we pick up the magazine that's lying on the coffee table. . . . If so much of our behavior is produced by our purely physical surroundings, we may well ask whether a self-management plan can include altering those surroundings in some way. And the answer, of course, is: Yes, it can. And has.

Some aspects of your environment have been set up in the interest of managing behavior, though you may never have thought about them that way. Your clock, for example. Imagine how confusing it must have been before there were clocks, how much time people must have spent waiting for others when appointments couldn't be made for precise times. Now almost everybody wears a wristwatch. We have alarm clocks and kitchen timers to get the message to us even when we are not looking at the clock.

So another rule of behavior management is: Analyze the physical environment. Note what behaviors it appears to call forth. Then make changes that will induce more desirable actions.

Vera thought of herself as a writer. She had once, ten years earlier, sold a story to a major literary magazine. She had not really written anything in a long time, however, which was the behavior she hoped to modify.

In discussing her physical environment, I inquired about her work area, how it was set up and where she kept the various things that she needed. She said that it was a beautiful room with a large window opening onto the grounds. There were many plants and a number of art objects, including several pieces of sculpture done by a friend of hers and a "magnificent" painting by her deceased husband. She spoke with great affection of the room. She said she spent a good deal of time there, just sitting in a favorite wicker rocking chair and looking out across the lawn. When I asked why she referred to the room as her "work area," she explained that in one corner of the room was her antique roll-top desk, painted white, with fresh flowers in old bottles on it, and in a nearby closet were her typewriter and file cabinets. Further questioning revealed that, to type, she had to remove the typewriter from its case and place it on the desk, where it was "too high, but I can manage it all right."

Evidently, Vera's room was very nice, but not for working. Later, she made that room her bedroom. She found that the drabness of her former bedroom was an advantage when it came to writing. She also traded her portable typewriter in for an office model that stood ever ready on a stand that she could easily pull over to her chair. In deciding what changes she wanted to make in her physical environment, she asked herself:

1. What do I usually do in that room?
2. What aspects of the room seem to call forth that behavior or those feelings?
3. What kind of physical environment would tend to induce the kinds of activities in which I wish to engage?

Using Gadgets and Modern Technology

Some people have a very strange attitude to getting help from objects. They resist it, preferring to do-it-the-hard-way—the old anti-coddle influence. To them such self-reliance seems closer to godliness.

I know what it's like; I went without an alarm clock for a few years. I have to admit there was a certain sense of control in being able to "do it myself." But it was really silly. One day, for some reason, I began to use a clock again, and I was amazed at what a marvelously helpful invention it was. It is a major part of self-management technology. And very helpful in regulating the schedule!

Here are some other common gadgets which can be of great help to self-managers:

A noise generator that masks sounds coming from elsewhere so you can sleep while others are up.

A kitchen timer to indicate when time is up or when it is time to carry out a certain act.

Earphones so that you can add music to a low-level task without disturbing others who are working nearby at higher levels.

A gate across the door to keep your two-year-old from falling down the stairs.

A tape recorder so that you can tape that radio program that comes on when you are Level One or Two. Your level is too high to listen now, but it will be just right later in the day when you are at Level Four. You can listen to the program in the evening while sewing.

A small notebook to carry around with you. All kinds of records can be kept in it. Better have a pencil, too.

Two pockets and a supply of paper clips or other small objects. If you want to count how many times you do something, just place one clip into the other pocket each time the behavior occurs. At the end of the day you'll know how many times you engaged in the act by counting the clips.

If some of these things seem super-obvious, that's the idea. We use anything and everything that we can think of that works. Some things are mundane; some are ingenious. Of course, we do not pretend to be original. A form of record keeping believed to have had an influence on the behavior of the record keeper was that old practice of carving notches on gun barrels. Or the quantity of shrunken heads hanging from the hunter's waist. Self-management is not new.

Here are some examples in which problems were solved through "technology."

When Gwen's husband, Walter, came home in the evening after work, he just wanted to do one thing: watch television. He would begin at six o'clock with the news and usually remained in his chair for most of the evening. Gwen joined him as soon as the dishes were done and their infant daughter had been put to bed. Gwen did not object to Walter watching television. The problem was that she could not watch the news except while eating. When she went into the kitchen, she could no longer see the television set.

The solution was simple. An electrician helped.

First, they rearranged the living room so that Gwen was able to observe the television screen as soon as she entered the room or from the hall. Second, auxiliary speakers were placed in the kitchen and in the baby's room so that Gwen could listen to the sound while she did her evening chores.

The following problem and solution were almost the exact opposite of what Gwen and Bill faced.

Zoe and Jim hated television, but felt that they could not deprive their son of his three or four favorite evening programs. The problem was that they would be more or less forced to watch also, because the apartment was small, and there was no place for the set except the living room.

The solution was to place the television set so that it did not dominate the room and to supply the child with earphones.

Technological solutions can help with all kinds of problems. A system of intercoms can help you monitor your children's playroom activities while you are in the kitchen. Or a speaker system can take sounds to any part of the house. Analyze the acoustics of your house or apartment and think about possible changes that would improve things.

In order to have an undisturbed period of creative work when she was at a high capacity level, Cynthia rose each morning at 5:00 A.M. Getting to bed no later than nine o'clock was a problem in a household including three teen-agers. She had tried earplugs and they helped. But if the children got loud in their discussion or if the telephone or doorbell rang, Cynthia often woke up and had great difficulty going back to sleep.

Her son Mike came home from high school one day with the newly acquired knowledge that "white" noise, noise that contains a wide range of frequencies, masks other types of sound. They were unaware that noise producers were manufactured just for this purpose, but they found a cheaper and equally effective method. They put a small, old AM radio beside Cynthia's bed, tuned between stations so that the noise of static was emitted. It took Cynthia a little while to quell her impulse to tune in to a station. But the radio was so effective in masking noise that soon she liked the sound.

The effective use of various gadgets and technological devices is a basic part of self-management. The main idea is that your attitude toward them should be positive and welcoming. Gadgets are good friends when used properly, so be ever on the lookout for ways in which they can assist you. It's another form of coddling yourself.

Don't Punish Yourself—Or Anyone Else, Either

None of the procedures recommended in this book involve the use of punishment. When I discussed changing your daily schedule so that something you would do anyway followed something you were trying to build up, I did not say that you should deprive yourself of the usual activity if you failed in the new behavior. If exercises are really important to you, the shower will be more enjoyable after the stint of exercising has been accomplished. You do not need to punish yourself by not having the shower (or meal or whatever). As we must continue to stress, reinforcement is the important principle in behavioral development. In self-management we arrange the situation so that good behaviors bring rewards (reforcements) in the form of increased satisfaction with ourselves and in discernible progress toward long-range goals.

Punishment can be effective. Much of what we do, in fact, is done to avoid punishment. We watch our fingers when we close car doors; we wait for the signal to cross the street; we count our change before leaving the bank teller's window; we put on snow tires—all these things are probably done to avoid unpleasant consequences of some kind. But punishment has unfortunate side effects. We try to escape anything associated with it if we can, and so it works best when escape is difficult or impossible. Punishment leads to anxiety, so it is not surprising that you do whatever you can to avoid situations in which it occurs.

These negative emotional reactions make it harder to change such behavior. There have, for example, been several such cigarette smoking plans based on punishment. You might receive a small electric shock whenever you touched a battery-operated cigarette case. Or, having placed a substantial sum of money in the hands of another person, you might lose a previously agreed-on portion of it to a hated organization (e.g., Sons and Daughters of Hitler or the K.K.K.) if the number of cigarettes you smoked exceeded a certain limit. Substances that make drugs (particularly tobacco and alcohol) produce nausea or other unpleasant side effects have also been used. But such punitive methods increase the chance that the person will simply walk away from the whole thing—leave the cigarettes out of the case that produces a shock or refuse to ingest the substances that make tobacco or alcohol unpleasant.

If we do not use punishment, you must be asking, how do we get rid of undesirable behaviors? The principle is: Strengthen alternative actions, especially alternative actions that are incompatible with the behavior to be weakened. If you feel that you talk too much, strengthen listening. If you fidget too much, strengthen sitting still. If you spend your money foolishly, strengthen saving. If you want to stop being late for appointments, strengthen being early.

And watch out for punishment that sneaks up on you in odd ways. You didn't really mean to punish, but it crept in. You forgot about coddling and started doing something the hard way, or you began to feel dissatisfied with progress and took too large a step. Failure to achieve a subgoal was then experienced as a punishment.

When we set deadlines for ourselves, we inadvertently risk setting ourselves up for unpleasantness if the goal is not reached. That's bad enough. Never add an additional punishment. Deadlines, despite the horrid name, can be useful if (1) they are self-determined well in advance of the ones set by others, and (2) if they are interpreted primarily as a reminder to feel joyful when they are met and serve as a warning signal when they are not. An unmet deadline is a signal to reevaluate the program. You may be asking too much of yourself, or unforseen circumstances may have interfered with your progress and necessitate a revised schedule. Never worry about changing a self-management plan. Coddling means taking the whole situation into account. It means that no unrealistic goals or subgoals are set, or held to once you know they're unrealistic.

Mary and Janet were working together on an article for a national magazine. Their schedule called for them to meet each weekday at nine o'clock in the morning for as long as they needed to in order to achieve a daily objective of a thousand words of final draft.

One day, after they had been working at the task only about an hour and were nowhere near completing the morning's work, Janet announced that she was quitting for the day. She explained that she had a headache and it was very difficult for her to continue. Furthermore, she feared giving their work unpleasant associations by pushing herself. She did not want to lose enthusiasm for the task. Fortunately, Mary knew enough about self-management to agree.

Self-management works only when it increases positive feelings. It should do this from the beginning, and continually. If your project is at all burdensome, go down to a smaller step.

Many writers on self-management recommend the use of contractual agreements in which you commit to paper what you plan to do, when you plan to do it, and what consequences you have arranged to follow improved behavior. Rewards of various sorts are stipulated when goals are met; if a goal is not reached, a punishing consequence may be planned. My students' experiences with contracts have made me wary of them. Circumstances may change; the unexpected may happen. In their relative inflexibility, contracts inhibit our freedom to change the plan as needed, and therefore to coddle.

Failures

Still, failures occur. Especially the first time around.

Be very patient with yourself on this issue. The failure is a failure *of the program as designed,* not of you. It is the program that goes back to the drawing board; not you. If you find that after all the analyzing and planning, when it comes right down to it you lose interest or inexplicably don't feel like carrying out the project, don't do it. Reevaluate. There are many things that may have gone wrong.

In my experience, the main cause of failure is trying to take too large a step. This usually happens out of eagerness to achieve long-range goals. That's certainly understandable, but remember that you begin where you are, not where you wish to go. Accurate baseline records are designed to show you were to begin, but sometimes the baseline records become inflated. Maybe wishful thinking influences record keeping and even the behavior itself.

Jeanne took baseline records on the amount she read per day. She was concerned about increasing her reading as part of a larger project designed to improve social skills.

When there was no improvement in the weeks following baseline, I suspected that maybe the baseline measure had been incorrect. It had. During baseline, Jeanne had been in the middle of a long but fascinating book of fiction. Afterward, she measured herself on reading newspapers, magazines about home improvement, and a less interesting novel. Although she was still measuring number of words read, the baseline task was different from the ones that followed and did not provide an adequate measure.

Margaret counted the number of cigarettes she smoked per day for three weeks of baseline recording. The range was from 5 to 20 cigarettes with an average of 15. During the first three weeks that her self-management plan was in effect, Margaret actually increased her average to 18 and never smoked fewer than 10 cigarettes. She was very distressed over this turn of events. The problem was that she had had a cold during baseline measurement, and this had caused her to smoke less often.

Using the principle of "small steps," set your first goals just above baseline; break tasks which are complicated and detailed into simpler chunks so as not to overwhelm yourself; and begin by taking on problems that are likely to bring success. The last means staying away from the most pressing problems because these are almost always too big a step for a new self-manager. Sometimes it is hard to select a behavior that meets all these criteria simultaneously. And sometimes in an effort to find an initial project that is not too large a step, you may choose something of insufficient importance.

Billie Ann's major worry at the time that she began her self-management project was that she had become exceedingly overweight. Her clothes no longer fit, she felt ugly, even grotesque, and she had been advised that she was risking severe health problems. The weight problem was so acute that it seemed inconsistent with the "small step" principle to tackle it as a first behavioral change.

After examining her situation in detail, Billie Ann selected finishing daily household chores earlier in the day as the goal of her first project. The daily tasks were specified and during two weeks of baseline observation it was found that it was usually not until late in the afternoon that they had all been accomplished. According to the plan, as soon as the chores were finished, Billie Ann would feel free to watch television, take a walk, or read.

But three weeks on the program produced little change in the time the chores were finished. It turned out that Billie Ann was fairly well able to control her impulse to eat while she was actually doing her housework, but when she relaxed, she could hardly stand not to be nibbling on something. With weight such a problem, eating between meals was something Billie Ann did not want to be encouraged to do. She actually did not want to finish her housework earlier because of this.

A new project in which she increased the amount of time she watched TV without eating was much more successful. And it was a "small step" because it dealt with only a limited aspect of the major problem.

A plan might need revision for many reasons. So be prepared to revise, and not to conclude that a setback or a temporary stalemate is a failure. Even after a plan has been in effect for a time and has produced some success, there may be problems. Sometimes a "plateau" is reached: the behavior has improved and the improvement is maintained, but that's where it has stopped, with no further improvement. We are not certain why this happens, but it is very common. It may be best just to sit it out.

Finally, your "failure" could be due to others sabotaging your efforts.

Gertrude wanted to get in earlier in the evening. During the baseline period her average was 12:30 A.M., which did not give time for sufficient rest. But after some initial improvement, she found the situation actually deteriorating. Her friends had begun to put additional pressure on her to stay out late.

You may suspect dark motives for such interference, but often it is just lack of understanding of the goals and methods of self-management. In such cases, it can help to bring the other person into the plan in a more positive way.

Lou's husband, Charles, seemed determined to undermine her attempts to stop smoking. He left cigarettes around more than he used to, or so it seemed to Lou. He gave her an expensive lighter for her birthday.

She revised the program. Instead of allowing herself additional reading time in the evening when she reached a subgoal in her smoking (something which Charles was not entirely happy with because he liked to have Lou join him in watching TV in the evening), she would add a certain amount of money to go into the evening meal. It could be used for wine, or for a more expensive cut of meat, dessert, or anything else that would make the dinner more luxurious. Thus, improvement in smoking led to rewards for both Lou and Charles. He stopped interfering. In fact, he began his own no-smoking plan.

Consummatory Behaviors

Acts which produce their own immediate rewards are the hardest to change. It is no accident that habits which we call "addictive" fall into this category. These are things which are gratifying in the short run, but prevent your achieving your long-range goals.

To manage consummatory behaviors by coddling, remove yourself as much as possible from situations that increase your tendency to engage in the behavior. Whenever the urge to engage in such behavior occurs, find substitutes to use.

Because Anna found that most of her cigarette smoking occurred when she was drinking coffee or alcoholic beverages, she avoided these substances during the initial period of abstinence. She used chewing gum as a substitute.

On the assumption that after several days of reduced intake, eating less would be easier, Carol began her diet by placing herself in an entirely new situation which contained very few food cues. She packed up only the amount of food that she allowed herself for the day and went off to the library, where she would read anything that happened to strike her fancy. If hunger became truly annoying, she took a half-hour off to go to the student center for a cup of coffee.

Whenever she was distracted by the thought of her former lover, Beth caught herself. She substituted by concentrating hard on her immediate surroundings until a new thought that was unrelated to her lover occurred to her. Gradually, she found herself freed from the obsession.

You can train yourself to substitute a new behavior by letting the urge to engage in the old behavior become the cue to the new behavior. For example, if you are trying to reduce eating sweets and drinking coffee and increase reading the newspaper, you might substitute the latter whenever you felt an impulse toward the former. A sign in the kitchen could be used to remind you of the substitute. But it is usually easier, especially at first, if the substitute is also a consummatory behavior.

Louise decided that she would stop smoking on May 2, two weeks hence. Before the date, she stocked up on substitutes like chewing gum and soft drinks. She permitted herself no visitors who would make the first days of abstinence difficult. She had already analyzed her smoking habit to find out what situations were the hardest without a cigarette. Those, she would simply avoid. She knew that after a week or so her craving would diminish enough for her to be able to remove some of the restrictions and treats.

By the third day, she no longer ate candy, but she still avoided certain social interactions and chewed a lot of gum. After four weeks, she was behaving almost normally, interacting without the impulse to smoke (or only very rarely did the impulse come, and it was easy to shake) and eating an excellent diet. The thing that lasted longest was the increase in the use of chewing gum, but eventually that was only after meals. Louise coddled herself by avoiding difficult social situations, allowing herself to eat candy, constructing an especially delightful and healthful menu, and more often engaging in activities just for fun—for example, reading detective stories. Although her work suffered some during the early part of the program, she had selected the boss's vacation time for carrying out her project. She knew she could make up for any lapses by the end of the month, when the boss would return.

Glenda found her "substitute list" very valuable, first in her weight-reduction program; later, when she stopped cigarette smoking. The list consisted of activities that she would try to engage in whenever she had an impulse to eat (or smoke). Some of the items on the list were:

> play the piano
> meditate
> write in my diary
> read a magazine
> walk around the block
> water the plants
> listen to one side of an LP record
> have a cup of tea or a glass of water
> go out to the garden and weed
> dust furniture
> make a telephone call

She would look over the list, select an activity that seemed suitable, and engage in it. Often the urge would go away as she engaged in the substitute behavior. If it didn't she'd select a second substitute, or if the urge was still very strong or persistent, she'd give in to it. As time went on, the urges were fewer and farther between.

Many people feel that they engage in undesirable consummatory behaviors as a reaction to stress or emotional upset. "I eat when something is bothering me." "I smoke when I am nervous." "I bite my nails when I am impatient or frightened." If this seems to be true of you, look for a substitute related to reducing the emotional state if you can manage it. For example, you might want to learn deep muscle relaxation techniques so that you can relax effectively when you are troubled with an unpleasant emotional reaction. Or you might find that it is helpful to imagine pleasant events. If you do, plan by preparing them well in advance, commit them to memory, and when you need them, bring them to mind one by one, over and over, until you feel less inclined to commit one of those consummatory acts you are trying to decrease.

Whenever Rhea became upset, instead of reaching for a cigarette, she went into her room, lay down on the bed, and practiced muscle-relaxing techniques. Then she would visualize her favorite scene, lying on the warm beach with children playing nearby and the noise of the crashing surf in the distance.

In summary, to help control your urges to engage in undesired consummatory behaviors, remove cues and antecedents to prevent temptation, and substitute other actions whenever the urge appears. To remind yourself to make the substitution, plant cues in the environment. But don't expect to "just do it." Remember small steps. You may not be able to use the substitute at first. A smaller step would be a more compelling and attractive substitute. Or, at first, you might try engaging in *less* of the consummatory behavior itself (a smaller snack, just five puffs on the cigarette). Be pleased with yourself for any step you take—even if it is a small one.

Working at the Highest Levels

Whether you are still a full-time student, or you are returning to the classroom for part-time study, you have probably found that some course work is essential to the attainment of your long-range goals. In the next few sections in this chapter, I will be focusing, for the most part, on the two tasks faced by most students: reading and writing. They can pose special challenges.

Writing is a Level One activity for almost everyone, even those who write professionally. That is because Level One is the level of widest focus, the level at which you are able to encompass the broadest range of thoughts and concepts, at which you are most likely to see things in a new and useful way. Reading can be at any level. You can probably read *TV Guide* at Level Five. But you probably need Level One for new and complicated material such as is found in many textbooks.

Remember that for most people Level One is elusive. If you are unaware that it exists and do not know how to look for it, you can miss it entirely. Some days it does not appear at all, and you cannot usually summon it at your bidding. The most productive people have learned to plan their lives so that they can make the most use of it should it appear. The poet's "muse" is Level One. The muse seems to come and go as if it were an actual creature. The poet knows how to wait for an appearance and be ready when it happens. The woman submerged under thirty pounds of Monday wash can scarcely rush to the typewriter in the middle of it all—especially when the baby's diaper is dirty and her four-year-old will be home from morning nursery school in half an hour. Virginia Woolf knew about these things when she observed that for a woman to write she needed an income and a room of her own. Distraction drives out the muse.

Using your top level in pursuit of a long-range goal is extremely pleasurable. And it is a psychological law that things associated with pleasant events seem positive in themselves. We *like* whatever has become associated with other pleasures. I think this is why productive people often become attached to a room, a view, furniture, or even clothing that is associated with times of high creativity.

Some psychologists advise that the work area be used for no other activities, because the chair, desk, and location become antecedents to work behavior if that is what has been associated with those things. Probably the best way to increase the chances of catching some Level One time is to put yourself in a situation in which Level One appeared in the past. That probably means getting into your work area and starting in.

Warm-ups

Assume that you have found the time of day in which your levels are usually highest, that you have managed to eliminate most sources of distraction, and you are settled into the chair and place associated with work. If with all of that going for you, you do not immediately begin top-level performance, don't be surprised or discouraged. It usually takes some period of time before the real work can begin. The time varies from person to person and from day to day in the same person. It is the time to engage in "warm-up" activities.

Exactly what good warm-up behavior is is so much an individual matter that you must discover what works for you. It might be sharpening pencils, watering plants, lying in bed thinking about where you will begin the work, a brisk walk, reading, writing in your journal, going over file cards, rereading and correcting yesterday's writing, staring out a window or at a wall, filing your nails, or meditating.

Some warm-up behavior is ritualistic. It occurs much the same way at the beginning of each work session.

Other warm-up behavior is more variable. It is good to give yourself up to whatever activities get you in the mood for work, so long as they do that and don't take over the work period. It is another strongly recommended way of coddling yourself.

But you may find yourself dawdling at the usual warm-up activities, staring longer at the wall, filing your nails down to the quick, or strongly tempted to pick up a magazine. When you feel strongly that you do not want to engage in a particular task, *do not force yourself.* Do not clench your teeth and approach the work with grim determination.

Finding an Entrance

Steel will and grim determination can succeed in getting you to perform a task only if the activity is of a sufficiently low level. Jogging a mile, scrubbing the kitchen floor, waxing a table top, cleaning the car, and even weeding the garden are all tasks that you can probably force yourself to do. The quality of the performance won't suffer greatly. But you'll suffer. And you won't like the work any better for it. You may come to like it even less than before.

Formerly unpleasant tasks can be made pleasant when they are done at an appropriate level. The opposite also holds true. Pleasurable activities can be made disagreeable when they are done at the wrong time. We are not interested in self-torture or exacting penance. We know that the task in which you take pleasure is the task at which your performance is top-rate. You will actually work better by coddling yourself.

But what should you do when you simply do not feel up to high-level activities? If a deadline is approaching, or if a long time has gone by unproductively, you can't simply switch to something you feel like doing and wait indefinitely for the muse to return. You are getting anxious about things, and everything that is not real progress feels lousy.

There is always the possiblity that you have truly set your sights too high, that the Great American Novel is not hidden away in your brain somewhere, that the task you hoped to accomplish is really beyond your ability even when you are at top levels. This is something you must answer for yourself, but in my experience the likelihood of this being the case is slight—especially with women. We are more likely to run at the first sign of trouble than to be unrealistic about our goals. Still, it is a possibility, and you will want to consider it.

Much more probably—and certainly so when you have already accomplished something but then have hit a snag or become blocked—some unknown difficulty is obstructing your *entrance* to the work. Your problem is to find a way in. Maybe by the back door.

Most tasks consist of a variety of specific activities at different levels. Do some of the lower-level things rather than leave the task altogether. It often happens that while doing them your level will suddenly rise. You will get an idea of how to solve the problem that is making the task difficult. Usually, when one is stuck, one is stuck on a problem for which a solution has not yet been found. Going to other aspects of the task while waiting for the solution to appear can be very helpful.

The noncreative person plods along doing "first things first" and never starts anything new until the previous task has been completed. That strategy leads straight to mediocrity. Creativity involves turning things upside down and looking at them from different angles. It involves mulling things over. It involves supreme sensitivity to your feelings and impulses. It involves self-trust. It involves not blaming yourself or feeling inadequate when things go badly and problems resist unraveling. It involves patience.

And it also involves staying *near* the task, if not quite at it. You can't find an entrance if you go too far away from the problem. Get as close as you comfortably can. And, as the following examples show, be sensitive to your reactions.

Jean, a dress designer, suddenly found herself stuck. She had, or so she thought, almost finished the garment she had been working on, but she was having peculiar difficulties with the final details. She tried one thing, then another, but nothing seemed to work. She began to get really annoyed because she was losing a lot of time on this one item and she had others to do. Finally, she abandoned it, at least temporarily, and went on to the rest of her assignment. Two weeks later, when she returned to it, the problem was glaringly obvious. The design was fundamentally flawed. To save it would require basic revision. She decided to scratch it, regretting only the time she had spent by not going on to other things sooner.

Lilian had hoped to finish her term paper three weeks before the end of the semester, but for the last few days she had not made any significant progress at all. She looked for an entrance by going over the incomplete manuscript for minor errors and stylistic improvement. Finding one sentence which seemed to need recasting to rid it of awkwardness, she spent twenty minutes trying out one thing after another. Suddenly it hit her. The content of that sentence was the problem. In it she tried to say something that she really could not justify on the basis of her research. That was what had been bugging her. With the sentence removed, the problem was solved and the rest of the writing proceeded smoothly.

Working around the problem rather than trying to attack it head on is often the fastest solution in the end.

Dealing with Anxiety

Getting stuck is often connected with anxiety. A main reason for getting things done long in advance of deadlines is that it helps to keep the anxiety down. Anxiety interferes with productivity; what might have been easy becomes difficult when the obstacle of anxiety must be overcome at every turn. Anxiety is fear, and the common types of fear surrounding work are: fear that it will not get done, fear that it will be done poorly, and fear that one is really incapable of succeeding at a selected goal. Anxiety makes us run at the first sign of difficulty; when we are ruled by anxiety, we interpret a minor setback as a major defeat.

Much of the coddling recommended in self-management is designed to keep anxiety down. It is especially important to avoid a vicious cycle in which anxiety prevents accomplishment, which is interpreted as evidence of unworthiness, which leads to more anxiety that further interferes with accomplishment. At the end of such a cycle you are totally incapacitated and productive work is impossible. You would be truly surprised at the many famous and productive people who have had bouts with such cycles. The well-known "writer's block" is probably an example of that process. For blocked writers, work has come to produce anxiety because it is not going well. But not working also produces anxiety. Many people escape that bind via intoxication. Drunk or stoned, the work doesn't exist anymore and the anxiety subsides, at least during the period of intoxication. But the effective way to overcome the anxiety that results from seeing that your long-range goals are going down the drain is to reverse the trend by managing yourself.

Your morale is very dependent on progress toward

long-range goals. Therefore it is important that the work you do today have a clear relationship to the ultimate accomplishment of those goals.

Louise was discouraged because she felt that she would never achieve her aim of becoming a journalist. Jobs were impossible to get, and she had finally settled for being a file clerk in a brokerage firm. The work was boring and she was underemployed. She talked with a friend of her father's who was a successful newspaper reporter and who advised Louise to write regularly and to submit her articles for publication in the local papers or other periodicals. She also advised her as to the kind of stories that would most likely bring some success.

Louise coddled herself by demanding very little in the beginning. She first found what seemed like the best time of day for work, then began to research a simple story that she felt would pose few writing difficulties, yet be of interest to the local newspaper.

Allowing herself to be satisfied with as little as fifteen minutes' work a day at first, she kept records of how much time was spent and how many words written. She vowed not to be upset if the amount was small as long as something was accomplished.

She worked first thing in the morning, before her shower. After a month, she was rising at 5:30 A.M. and spending up to two hours at each work session. Long before she was able to get any favorable reaction from others, she had become pleased with herself and the progress she was making. When, after four months, she received an acceptance, she was overjoyed. Furthermore, her pattern of regular working had been established once and for all.

The strategy of taking small steps often means scheduling a small amount of time. But sometimes it may also mean working at a simpler level or in a manner that is easier for you.

Bette was getting absolutely nowhere with her writing. The anxiety level had increased to the point where she had begun to find anything that reminded her of writing to be anxiety-producing. It made her nervous to look at the typewriter.

The behavioral counselor with whom she consulted helped her to set up a plan that would help decrease her anxiety about writing while she also made progress. Bette was to use the typewriter for writing letters, making lists of things to be done around the house, and even for writing checks. But at first she was not to attempt the *real* writing, at least not with the typewriter. She used the tape recorder technique of first talking into the recorder in a loose and free-flowing way, just getting her thoughts on the subject of her writing down in some form. When she listened to the tape, she noted down in longhand the points she felt were worthwhile. She rearranged the list and retaped. The second time the points were made in better form, and other aspects of them began to be developed. Since she was still not ready for the typewriter, she taped a third time. With this taping, she practically had her article written.

Anxiety lowers your level. The task must be made easier, which is what using the tape recorder accomplished. For most people, as it was for Bette, talking is easier than writing, especially when you are uncertain about just what you want to say. Using a tape recorder to coddle yourself that way is likely to be very helpful.

The tape recorder can also help students who are unable to study because of the unpleasantness that has come to be associated with certain course work. The closer they get to their books, the more intensely they feel anxiety. Anxiety has pushed the level down to the point where it is very hard to function.

Alberta was so upset over her poor grades that she had come to hate school altogether. She was going downhill fast. She complained that as soon as she sat down at her desk, she would feel ill or tired. She had a history examination coming up in a week and she knew nothing at all. To pass would mean memorizing names and dates and places—hundreds of them. She felt it was no use; there was nothing that could help her.

Ms. Warren, her high school counselor, explained how the tape recorder could be made into a kind of teaching machine. First, Alberta was to record questions taken right out of her history book. After asking herself a question, she was to leave enough time on the tape to give the answer, then put the answer on the tape and go on to the next question.

Setting up the tape was easy because it required no memorization in itself. The next day, when she listened back, Alberta supplied as many answers as she could during the blank periods following the questions. At first, she knew none of them. But by the fourth or fifth time around, she had really learned some history.

Summarizing the Ways to Increase Productivity

The first and most important principle for increasing productivity in relation to your work is to *take yourself and your work seriously.* Set your sights realistically high. Assume that you can do things that you have never done in the past. Make room in your life for true accomplishment. *See to it that each day brings some discernible progress toward the long-range goals.* This is very important in keeping anxiety down and morale up. Don't be afraid to *proceed in very small steps.* You'll get there.

Recognize that serious work will ultimately mean some restrictions on the time you spend on leisure and entertainment. But this will not be experienced as a deprivation if you are at the same time beginning to enjoy the work itself and deriving the satisfaction that comes from having done it.

Coddle yourself by using any gadget or technological device that can help, by making the steps as small as necessary, and by being very sensitive to your levels so that you do not push yourself to do what is too much for you at any given moment. Quit before it begins to hurt. What is impossible today might be easy tomorrow.

Set deadlines so far in advance that you can always afford a poor workday without becoming anxious. When one occurs, try to *find an entrance* through working on the periphery at a lower level or switching to another work in progress. There is probably no task that does not involve work at several levels, even Level Five. Sweeping up under your desk, emptying the wastebasket, and cleaning the typewriter are all low-level tasks that will improve the work atmosphere and maybe make things easier tomorrow. Your book will not be written in a day, but if you do something every day, it will be written.

Setting Realistic Standards

I have talked mostly about quantity in this chapter. But what about that nagging fear that even though the novel is written, it will not get published because it is no good? So I'm writing two thousand words a day, but they are unreadable. What about that? What about the anxiety that comes from self-doubt, from the feeling that all this work is really going nowhere? Maybe you might just as well be watching television as knocking yourself out under the delusion that you will produce something the world will want, when what you're doing is actually only fodder for the wastebasket.

To protect yourself from the ultimate failure that would occur if your work were lacking in quality, it is important that you test reality from time to time—both the reality of your own later reactions and those of others whom you respect. The person who spends five years writing a book which no one sees until it lands on the publisher's desk is taking needless risks. True, it has worked out all right for some writers that way—maybe any other way would have failed—but for most people it could be a disaster. Although it is probably true that our greatest artistic contributors have had to work in the relative isolation that comes from being ahead of their time, their isolation was rarely truly absolute. We need the support of others. Their evaluation of our work helps us set our own standards. On the other hand, the principle of small steps should apply here, too.

When Flora received her twentieth rejection slip, she felt that she had hit bottom. She despaired of ever being successful, and she began to work intermittently, and finally not at all. A few months later at a party someone asked her about her work and she explained that she had given it up and why. She was talking to a successful writer who questioned her about the details of those submissions and rejections. He laughed. She had sent her stories only to the biggest magazines in the country.

He explained that those magazines very rarely accept work from unknown writers and that even if her work was of the quality they would usually publish, the chances of their accepting anything of hers were exceedingly small. They probably had not even read what she sent. He said that despite the fact that he had had articles published in major magazines, he also had received many rejections—many more than twenty. When Flora told him that she knew her material had been read at least once—she received one personal letter saying that while they could not accept the present work they would like to see any other article she might write—her friend said that she should feel very encouraged. She was also advised to submit her work to smaller publications, where the competition would not be so stiff.

There is also the danger that you will set too high standards for yourself too early. Ultimately, high standards are important, but many of us tend to be supercritical when it comes to what we have produced ourselves compared to how we judge the work of others. I have saved this point for stressing toward the end of the chapter because it is so important. Again, I will illustrate with an example about writing although the principle to be derived from the example applies to any form of creative work.

Zoe had a concept of perfectly flawless writing. She would struggle with each word and phrase and not want to go on to the next sentence until she was totally satisfied with the one before it. Often, she would work so hard on one sentence that she would lose touch with the major points she was trying to make. She did very little writing and almost nothing she felt satisfied with.

Coddling and going in small steps means allowing for error and imperfection and for successive approximations of the satisfactory final product. Of course you must continually evaluate your work, but allow your standards to vary depending on what phase of a project you are on at the moment. Let a draft be very rough at first. It's enough to get down a couple of good basic concepts and strategies. Don't worry about some awkward wording and unfinished sections at the outset. Assume that those will be taken care of later. Let some time go by.

Read what others say about their working habits; you can pick up ideas that way. But know that you will work out your own method, one that will differ from everyone else's in that it reflects you and your unique situation.

Overcoming Small Hurdles and "Being Lucky"

There are two more general concepts that you might find useful in your self-management projects. The first involves recognizing that often a small but annoying obstacle to further progress develops that must be overcome then and there. Learning a better way often means temporarily not performing quite as well as you did by the old methods. That's the hurdle.

Cynthia played the piano rather well, but she was not improving. The trouble was with fingering. She had to stop and learn her fingering. This meant not being able to breeze through her pieces as she had been doing, but it was the only way to achieve further progress.

The same thing applies to typewriting and to many other skills. Watch out for this stage. It's a shame to be forever stuck on the other side of such an obstacle. Accept the temporary slowdown, knowing that it is part of the process of real improvement.

The other principle can be stated in the form of the old saying that every cloud has a silver lining. As the following examples show, the idea is to turn troubles into "luck" whenever you can.

Martha was very ill for several months. However, she ended up not only recovered but at precisely the weight she had hoped to be.

Lisa Smith's house burned down. It was a tragedy that she lost virtually all her possessions. She decided to be much more careful about accumulations in the future. Although some of the things destroyed were very precious to her, others were things she found she was better off not burdened with.

If Sue had not lost her job, she might have stayed with the same company for the rest of her working life. The new job was a great improvement, and she is now grateful for what seemed a major setback at the time.

We cannot always direct the course of events, not even those that affect us deeply. But we can be always vigilant for pulling advantage out of adversity. Some people would call it luck. It's not. It's self-management.

Self-Managing
Your Problems
Away

The Self-Management High

As we have seen, self-management means getting yourself to do whatever you want to have done. You use the strategies detailed or suggested in this book, advancing day-to-day by little steps toward long-range goals. The control you will achieve over your actions can add up to a major change in your life, a change definitely for the better.

Don't hesitate to take on additional goals and projects. Be on the lookout for new behaviors to add to your repertoire and for ways of changing or eliminating those that are undesirable. The only restriction is to take on only what is possible at the time. Always watch for new things to modify, new heights to reach, by small successful steps.

Utilize whatever comes along that can help. The rejected lover spurns food in her misery; she also recognizes a propitious time to begin a weight-reduction plan. An employee who is laid off utilizes the new-found free time to begin a different career. Use opportunities to make transitions to new patterns.

Eventually it will get easier to find new things to work

on. When you first consider things that might be changed, avoid the seemingly impossible. Later, when some management has been achieved, things you would never have dared to think of tackling become matter-of-fact possibilities.

So stay flexible, and new objectives will emerge. Accomplishment gives rise to ambition.

Self-Managing Housework

It is the rare woman who is not a homemaker. We not only live in our homes, but their care is primarily our responsibility. Husbands, children, lovers, and occasionally paid employees "help" us sometimes, but the job is ours. Like it or not, we usually have the final responsibility for whether the dishes are done, whether the place has been vacuumed, or what's for supper.

If there is one thing that characterizes housework in general, it is the total failure of those for whom it has never been the sole responsibility to ever notice that it has been done. A freshly made bed is taken for granted; the unmade bed causes eyebrows to rise. The same goes but only more so for a clean kitchen sink. Even more cruel is the tendency of people to generalize. If the house is clean five days a week, but messy on two, the impression of messiness, not orderliness, will be left in people's minds. Credit for housework is hard to get.

Not long ago I did some research on communes, those multiple living arrangements that became popular in this country and in Europe in the sixties. There are many different kinds of communal living arrangements, but I was interested mainly in one thing: who did the dishes. There were several patterns. One commune operated on a labor credit system in which chores were valued in accordance with demand. The unpopular jobs were given more credit so that one could choose to work a longer time at a pleasant task or a shorter time at something more unpleasant. Doing the dishes was so unpopular that the system broke down. They had to set the time so low for it that there were not enough people to fill up all the work slots. Ten individuals willing to work five minutes a day on dishes was not enough to get the task done because it took about two hours a day to wash all the dishes and pots needed to feed that number. The group finally decided to place "dishwasher" at the top of its priority list of items to be purchased despite the low supply of funds.

When I was working full-time, writing my dissertation, and dealing with three young sons, someone once asked me how I managed it all and I very seriously said, "Paper plates." That he thought I was joking, or just using a metaphor, is not surprising. As a male, he had largely escaped the dishwashing fate. But of all the labor-saving devices I developed in those days, paper plates was probably the single most important one. They may have seemed an extravagance to some, an indelicacy to others; to me, it was a matter of simple survival.

For most of us, household tasks are at Level Four or even Level Five. They are repetitive in the extreme, and boring when we are at average or upper levels. They are also fatiguing. And one can always find more to do. Maybe the best that can be said for housework is that it is "challenging." The challenge is in getting it done without losing your sanity. In fact it can be planned, systematized, and self-managed into something which is tolerable even if it never gets to the point where it elicits any joy.

Because housework looms seductively everywhere we look, it is crucial to plan lest we succumb to fugue-ism. In psychological jargon, a fugue is a form of behavior.

It's not counterpointed melodic lines, my favorite form of music; it refers instead to a pattern of behavior which is associative, in which one thing leads to another. I start out for a walk, see a bus and take it, get off and go into a movie theater that happens to be in my path, leave the theater and find myself in the subway whose entrance was across the street from the theater exit. On the subway, I meet a friend and we go somewhere for a drink together. And so on. The sequence can go on indefinitely until something (like night, with all the shops and restaurants and bars closed up) brings it to a halt.

Do you ever have a kitchen fugue? You clear the table and put the dishes in the dishwasher, clean off the cabinets, notice that the walls are dirty and wash them, then the windows and floor, then clean out the cupboards, polish the silverware, and suddenly find three hours have gone by. Or four, if you decide while you are about it to scrape the wax from the floor. Sometimes housecleaning fugues are goof-offs in disguise. I'll never forget the fantastic scrubbing I once gave the kitchen floor when I was supposed to be writing an article for a psychological journal. It was virtually unconscious on my part; only after the job was finished did I realize what had happened. By then, of course, my journal-article-writing levels were exhausted. I had used them up in happy fantasy while I squeezed the dirty water out of the sponge mop.

The sad truth is that while the only thing you can really do at Level Four is a Level Four task, at Level One you *can* do anything you can do at any other level as well as the precious "more" that is unique to your Level One. If you are engaged in a Level Four task when your head is at Level One, daydreams—especially creative daydreams—may be used to bridge the levels gap. I had some great ones that day, I'm sure. All I remember is the clean floor and the unfinished article. I have since learned to recognize excessive housecleaning for what it really is—a tempting escape.

To avoid this, the thing to do is to plan your housework. This consists mainly of (1) making sure that things that must get done do get done and (2) limiting yourself.

And, of course, all the other self-management principles also apply.

Michael, whose wife, Nell, works full-time, and who fulfills the role of househusband by taking care of most household chores and of Lindy, three, and Robby, five, found that major household chores such as cleaning out the basement, washing the back stairs, and cleaning the stove were being neglected. The problem was that the neglected chores consumed a relatively large block of time. You simply cannot leave the stairs half-washed, or the stove half-cleaned, or the dishes lying out of the cupboards.

With two preschoolers in the home, it was no wonder such things were difficult. Michael made a list of major chores and divided the chores into those which could and could not be accomplished with the children underfoot. The schedule analysis revealed that the best times for engaging in these large tasks were (1) while the children napped, (2) in the evening, or (3) on the weekend, when there were two adults in the house. He also decided that cleaning out the basement was something the children could actually help him with, and, if a child-initiated emergency occurred while they were at it, that particular job could be interrupted and finished later.

Using the principle of planning, Michael set up regular times for doing the major household tasks. For example, he decided to do the stove on the following Wednesday evening at eight o'clock while Nell watched a television program of which he was not especially fond; during that time he could also listen to a symphony on the kitchen stereo. During the time between deciding when to clean the stove and the actual doing of it, Michael had time to (1) decide on and purchase his cleaning equipment, (2) give his wife sufficient warning that he would be unavailable for anything else during that time, and (3) pick out the musical selections he would play for himself while he worked.

Michael later reported that cleaning the stove was one of his favorite activities. It was done while he was at about Level Four—good for listening to music while doing a manual chore that required little thinking.

Although Michael did not need to take baseline records on the major household chores that he selected as his initial goals, his records describing his progress were useful in setting other goals.

Michael kept a list of the major tasks he intended to do and, as they were taken care of, he noted the date and time that they had been done and the amount of time it had taken him to complete each one. Eventually, he set up a schedule for those household chores to be done on a regular basis. In the meantime, he discovered another problem.

Dinner was often too late. Not only did the lateness annoy Nell when she came home from the office tired and hungry, but it made the children cross. Furthermore, there was too little time after dinner for cleaning up and bathing the children.

Two weeks' baseline data showed that dinner was served as early as 5:00 P.M. (which was the time they had initially agreed on) and as late as 7:30 P.M. Seven times during baseline measurement it was after six-thirty. Rather than declare that from now on dinner would always be on time, Michael set his initial goal more realistically through the use of the baseline information. An interim goal was not to be later with dinner than six forty-five.

Some things cannot be avoided. They must be done if life is to continue in relative comfort. This disgusting truth is mitigated only by the fact that most people count things as essential that total efficiency would rule "optional." When you consider what could possibly (1) be reduced to a considerably smaller task, (2) be done less often, (3) be done in a shorter period of time, or (4) be accomplished well enough at a lower level, you might find that the things that cannot be avoided are reduced considerably.

For two weeks, Glenda observed herself and took notes. She found that she spent an average of seven hours per day engaged in some form of housecleaning or food preparation. Each morning, she made the family's four beds, washed the breakfast dishes, picked up in the living room and family room, dusted, watered the plants, and planned the evening meal. In the afternoon, she shopped, visited with friends, and sometimes took a nap before she began to prepare the dinner, which was always served at exactly six-thirty. Heavier housecleaning was done by a paid worker who came in once a week. Occasionally, on weekends, the entire family joined in a major project such as cleaning the basement or reorganizing one of the children's rooms.

Glenda had begun to feel that her time was not being used well. The youngest of her three children was now ten years old and she wanted to try to establish some identity outside of her housekeeper role. Specifically, she hoped to find a job in her old field, fashion merchandising. The question now was whether she could manage to have the household run smoothly when she was away from home all day. Up until now she had dismissed the idea out of hand. But the relationship between her and her husband had deteriorated from what it once had been and even divorce could not be ruled out. She wanted to be prepared.

Analysis of the household chores suggested many major changes: (1) family members would take on responsibility for making their own beds, taking their own clothes to the laundry room, and picking up in the family room; (2) the evening meal would still be planned by Glenda, but a week in advance so that all the shopping could be done on one evening by her husband and the older children; and (3) the youngest child would be paid for watering the plants every day after school. Thus Glenda's seven hours a day were reduced. She was amazed at how easily her tasks could be dispensed with.

Although Glenda's situation may seem an extreme example of someone spending her days engaged in essentially unnecessary tasks, some degree of this inefficiency is very common to the way many women approach housework. Then they find, as children grow older, that their mother/housewife function has gradually changed. Sometimes, services that had once been essential to family members may be continued for other reasons.

Greta spent two hours a day caring for her indoor garden and plants. They were beautiful and she found the time spent on them both relaxing and pleasurable. What had begun as a minor aspect of housecleaning had developed into a genuine interest. When she returned to part-time employment, she got up earlier in the morning so that she could continue to put in those two hours each day.

But most women who manage households have little time for increasing the family's nonessential pleasures. They are trying desperately to finish what they feel must be done before bedtime each day. When their situations are analyzed, it becomes a matter of very carefully deciding what can be changed in the routine in order to reduce their load.

Vera lived in a two-bedroom apartment with Virginia and Edith, her seven- and twelve-year-old daughters. She was a schoolteacher, and the three of them left and returned each day at about the same time. Vera complained of a chronic feeling of fatigue (she could not finish her lesson plans because she would fall asleep over them), too much housework to do, and lack of cooperation on the part of her children.

The first thing that helped was the levels analysis. It was discovered that by the time dinner was done and the kitchen cleared, Vera's level was too low for her to be able to prepare her lessons for the next day. Since she reached a high level early in the morning, she arranged to rise an hour earlier and do that task in the morning. She was delighted to find that although she had been spending as much as three hours on it in the evening, she never needed more than an hour to do it when she was fresh.

Further changes eliminated some chores (they gave the cat away), reduced the time spent on others (eating week-night meals in the kitchen rather than the dining room saved steps and time), and moved certain things to the weekends (vacuuming and dusting the living room, cleaning the bathroom, and washing the kitchen floor were not only moved to Saturday, but were done every two weeks, rather than weekly).

Success in getting the cooperation of Virginia and Edith was more involved and took more time, but it, too, was eventually managed.

Caring for one's home tends to be idiosyncratic. We have certain things that we are very particulary fussy about and other things that don't bother us at all.

Marianne and Bill were fiends about dust—especially dust under the bed or in the bedclothes. Every night before retiring, Bill dusted the bedroom floor and wiped under the bed with a damp mop. In the morning, the bedclothes were hung outside to air while they ate breakfast.

Vivian could not bear a dirty sink. No matter what else was out of place or uncleaned, the kitchen sink sparkled. She cleaned it every night just before she went to bed.

Sue was neat, some thought excessively so. There was never a magazine out of place in her living room, a dish in the sink. On the other hand, her house was not particularly clean if one looked closely. Dirt did not bother her. Ashtrays, for example, would be emptied but unwashed. There were dust rolls under the furniture. The kitchen counters were clear, but somewhat grimy.

Lisa's apartment was so messy that its condition was a standard joke among her friends. It was said that she once spent three days searching for her eyeglasses during which time she uncovered three hundred dollars in loose change and forgotten bills, eight library books for which she had already paid fines, and an old boyfriend. But Lisa's kitchen was spotless. She was fastidious about anything that came in contact with the food she ate.

Housecare is culturally conditioned. Much of what we experience as our individual preferences has actually been learned as part of our cultural heritage. In this society, daily or weekly cleaning is considered standard, and TV commercials and furniture store displays suggest a kind of spotlessness that may be more harmful in its effects on our life-style than healthful for the microbes it removes. One can tolerate having a few germs around.

Lillian had learned to cut a lot of corners in managing a home, job, and three children. But she never once questioned the necessity of a thorough household cleaning once a week. It was after the children were grown that she once allowed her house to go for six weeks without the floors being cleaned and was astonished by the fact that some dire catastrophe did not occur. The floors became dirtier, but not nearly as much as she would have expected. Of course, the fact that there were no children in the house meant that the kitchen floor was not muddy and cracker crumbs did not accumulate to attract rodents and insects. Still, she found it remarkable that visitors did not even seem to notice. After that, Lillian did some reevaluating. She vacuumed every three weeks instead of every week.

Being very stingy about how much time we want to spend on housework can lead us to make some radical changes in routine. What, really, are the daily musts? Making the bed? Well, sometimes not even that.

Louise began not making the beds. She realized that the bedrooms were empty all day long because every member of the family worked or went to school. The bedrooms were used only for sleeping and changing clothes. She had wanted to present the image of a perfect house. She realized that that was impractical, in fact silly. She did make the beds when weekend guests came. Otherwise, she even stopped apologizing if anyone happened to get a glimpse into the bedrooms.

On the other hand:

Bea hated bed making, but there was no way of avoiding it. She lived in a one-room apartment and her bed was also her couch.

Eating and personal grooming would seem excellent candidates for the status of daily "musts." But the manner in which these things are accomplished can be changed so that even they consume less time and energy.

To cut down on food-preparation time, the Browns decided to eat out twice a week, once at the neighborhood fish 'n chips place and once at one of the city's moderately priced restaurants. On a third night, they purchased a prepared ready-to-eat meal either from the fried chicken shop or from the Chinese restaurant. They held a home "feast" once either on Saturday or Sunday, and the rest of the time they ate meals prepared in what had been their usual way.

Martha and Ruth, who shared an apartment, stopped having meals altogether. Both were trying to lose weight, and it had been recommended to them that a painless way of shedding pounds was to forgo meals. Instead they could munch on nutritious high-protein and vegetable snacks whenever they felt hungry. Six months later, they were several pounds thinner and had given up meals forever (except for special occasions). They had discovered that eating independently of one another had many advantages. Their schedules did not always coincide, and it took much less time to get an apple or some yogurt and simply eat it than to bother with table setting and all the rest of what went into eating jointly.

Some of our household practices may be said to represent a kind of cultural lag. Things that made sense at one time are continued despite the fact that they have become unnecessary and even burdensome. Ritualized eating is a good example, and it may also have a lot to do with the high incidence of obesity in modern industrialized countries.

Eating independently of other members of the family has many advantages. It permits flexibility and reduces overeating. With prepared foods readily available and easy to heat up, dishwashers to place dishes and utensils in, and large refrigerators and freezers in most homes, it is only custom that has prevented it from becoming a widespread practice sooner.

Leah and Marc, her fifteen-year-old son, shared a two-bedroom apartment. They never ate together except occasionally in a restaurant. The refrigerator was kept stocked with fruit, ready-to-eat vegetables such as carrot sticks and celery, cold cuts, cheese, bread, cookies, and juices. About two or three times a month, Leah would cook a large roast—sometimes beef or lamb, but Marc was especially pleased when it was a turkey. The system worked very well.

Many families have adopted the independent pattern for breakfast, and many others have applied it also to weekend lunch.

But there are noneating functions of joint meals to be reckoned with. Through drama and literature, if not through actual experience, we are all familiar with the scene in which the father sits at the "head" of the table and the mother serves. The children, lined up along the table's sides, must arrive with evidence of recent hand-washing and be prepared to answer questions on current events. Report cards might lie nearby, awaiting discussion over dessert. Resolution of such questions as whose turn it is to mow the lawn might be undertaken by the patriarch. (Although one might wonder whether a meal is the optimum time during which to deal with such issues, this seems to be a fairly typical American custom.) A separate eating area such as a dining room or alcove is required for full development of the pattern. Women (wife and daughters) scurry about, in and out of the kitchen. Eating can begin only after all the expected persons have taken their places. All in all, the pattern adds many "musts" compared to that of independent eating. For example, after the meal there is a large cleaning-up to contend with.

Buffets combine independent with joint eating. They have become so popular for entertaining that "sit-down" dinner parties are now rare. One of the greatest advantages of a buffet is that it uses the labor of all diners in the serving of the food. It also provides greater flexibility with respect to individual diets. I am personally impressed with the freedom one has at a buffet *not* to eat certain foods and quantities. At a formal dining table, one may often eat out of sheer boredom while waiting for others to finish. You are "stuck" in your chair with all those antecedents to eating before you. At buffets, the dieter need not apologize or explain. And with everybody up and about, serving themselves, those who serve the food seem less like servants. These advantages apply to family meals, as well as meals with guests.

If you feel you may be doing more housework than you really need to, analyze each household task by asking yourself the following questions: How much labor would I save if I altered the pattern? What real function does it serve?

When Brenda considered those questions in her housework analysis, she discovered that much of her labor was in the service of promoting her image of a Superwoman, one who feels compelled to succeed superlatively at all traditionally female functions. Each day she made five beds, prepared and served three meals, and cleaned with a vengeance.

The problem is that Superwoman is doomed to eventual layoff as the family matures. Moreover, the woman who seeks identity through managing an outstanding household is likely to get much less recognition than her efforts deserve, or than the same energy output would receive if it were spent in pursuit of some other identity.

Usually, the best we can do is to be as efficient as possible. This often means setting definite limits.

Virginia reorganized her whole approach to her household tasks. She would not allow herself to spend more than a certain period of time at housecleaning. She decided that in order to maintain her three-room apartment according to ordinary standards, she would spend no more than an average of two hours a week on the heavier cleaning and twenty minutes a day on the dusting and "straightening."

After a month, she decided that she had allowed too much time. The limitation had caused her to work so much more efficiently in the time available that one and a half hours per week for "heavy" tasks proved more than adequate.

Setting time limits prevents fugues and causes one to get more done in the allotted time. The attitude becomes: "Anything I can't get done in this time goes undone unil next time."

Planning increases efficiency. When the brain knows

something is coming up, it prepares. Items to be put on the list of things to do during the next housecleaning interval will occur to you at odd times—in the shower, immediately on awakening in the morning, or while riding on the subway. Something sets up a train of associations and you find yourself remembering that you are running low on dishwasher detergent or that the tool chest needs organizing. If you carry pen and paper (choose one of those notebooks that come in various small sizes), you will be able to get down the thought and then you can rest assured that the task will be done when the times comes. One small notebook can be used for everything—list of ideas, supplies to purchased, and so on. It has the advantage of not getting lost the way individual pieces of paper might. Another approach is to place paper and pencil at strategic places in the house so that running lists of groceries, bathroom supplies, letters that should be written, telephone calls to be made, or any other similar reminders are conveniently at hand.

Sometimes planning a grocery shopping trip requires fairly complex logistics. Which store should I go to first? If I go to the fish store before the supermarket, the fish may spoil from being in the hot car while I do the other shopping. When are the stores most and least crowded? Is it too early in the week to purchase the meat for Saturday's guests? Such decisions may tax a brain operating at low level, but be easy to make at other times.

Lists enable you to enjoy one of life's purest pleasures: crossing items off. After a task has been accomplished, the list is visibly reduced by those glorious lines drawn through words that had represented tasks to be done. Now the crossed-off words mean tasks one need no longer be concerned with.

Miriam explained that her notebook provided encouragement when things got jammed up because she needed only to flip back to other lists of weeks and months ago in which items had been entirely crossed off. This let her know once again that there might be a lot to do, but that it all would get done in time with planning.

The old lists represent records of progress like a weight chart or any other graph. And they also provide reinforcement for tasks accomplished.

In planning housework, we should also remember that how the environment appears is important to most of us.

Mary had learned to do very little housecleaning. She lived alone, had no pets, and there were no children running in and out. She found that heavy cleaning about once every six weeks was sufficient to meet her new standards. But she did keep things neat. She had fresh flowers whenever possible. She also kept her mirrors and glass table tops sparkling. It required little effort, and it made the apartment seem as if it were freshly cleaned.

Scrubbing the kitchen floor could go unnoticed, but the condition of the glass table top was immediately obvious. So give more attention to what shows.

Ruth's view of the river was spectacular. Guests were immediately drawn to the window as soon as they entered the room. Taking advantage of this, Ruth kept that window spotless. Dust elsewhere was much less noticeable.

Another way of putting it might be: Little things mean a lot. If you don't believe that, take a Sunday newspaper and put its sections around an otherwise uncluttered room. Then pick them up. See what I mean? Now some of you will prefer the room *with* the newspaper spread around. Some people prefer a certain degree of clutter. But no one wants uncontrolled clutter that leaves no chair free to be used or that makes it impossible to walk without stepping on things.

"Self"-Managing Children

It has been found that the nature of the physical home environment has much to do with the behavior of children. So when a problem arises, study your situation carefully before you decide what to do about it.

Mary's four-year-old son, Abraham, was incorrigible when it came to tracking dirt and mud on the kitchen floor. Mary continually requested that he remove his boots before he came inside the house, but Abraham kept "forgetting." Analysis of the situation revealed that (1) the boots were very difficult to remove, and (2) especially in a standing position. Mary bought her son larger-size boots for play and placed a little bench just outside the kitchen door for him to sit on while he took them off. Result: problem solved.

Who shares a bedroom with whom can have complex ramifications. The formula commonly used is to put the older children in rooms of their own and to double up the little ones. Children of the same sex usually room together. But in certain situations, deviations from this pattern may work better.

The Smith family consisted of Gladys and her five children: Susan, twelve; Lily, ten; Brian, seven; twins Brad and Lewis, five; and the "baby," Ginger, one and a half. Gladys worked nights as a nurse, and her mother came in daily to care for the children. The Smiths' apartment contained only three bedrooms. Gladys and Ginger shared one of them, Susan and Lily shared another, and the three boys had the third. All three bedrooms were the same size.

One of the main problems was the continual bickering between Brian and his younger brothers. Although he was older, the twins usually agreed with one another and sided against him. Fights were often over Brian's books. The twins would tear out pages, write in them, and even hide them. Reprimanding the boys had no effect whatever.

The solution was to have Ginger and Brian change places. The twins went to bed at about the same time as Ginger, so there was no problem there. The great advantage was that not only were Brian's possessions protected by being located in his mother's room, but he was able to find peace and quiet for reading and doing homework there during the daytime.

Children need space. Generally, the younger the child, the more space needed. At various ages, children also need different kinds of space in different locations. The toddler's main requirement is that the play space be near where Mommy or other adults are working.

When Judy was first learning to crawl, her parents, Jane and Rod, decided that they could manage with a little less kitchen cabinet space. They removed the door to the lower cabinet in the corner (away from the stove and out of the main traffic patterns), exposing the shelves. Then they displayed Judy's favorite items plus some dispensable kitchen equipment. While her parents cooked and washed up, Judy was able to play happily and safely a few feet away.

The way a child behaves, at any age, will be greatly influenced by the physical space and available equipment in the home.

Parents often complain that their children do not play in the area of the house allotted for play. But they will if it is made rewarding for them to do so. They will more easily get into the habit of putting their toys away, too, even as very little children, if this is made easy to do by providing a place for their things, and if they are rewarded for doing so in small steps.

Dorothy realized that simply providing her children with good play equipment was not enough to ensure that they made good use of it. She had too often seen homes in which excellent equipment was wasted because it was not cared for with respect.

Not only did Dorothy provide equipment, space in which to use it, and shelves on which to store it, but she taught her children how to keep their play area in order. At first, she would work along with the children, making the pick-up task smaller and being right there to reward small steps. As they became more capable, she withdrew her assistance. The process was so gradual that it took place over several months.

The order of the instructions is crucial. "You can go out now if you promise to do your homework later" sounds reasonable enough, and on rare occasions may work out all right, but if you use it as a general rule you will have problems. Always present the sequence so that the more pleasant event takes place after the less pleasant one. Say, "When you have your play clothes on, you may go outside," and, "After you do your homework you may watch television for an hour." Just as you place activities in a hard-easy or more-difficult/less-difficult order for yourself, do the same for your children. This rule applies not only to orderliness, but to everything you want them to do.

Effective child care also means being on hand to prevent undesirable behavior from occurring and somehow getting rewarded. The younger the child, the closer you must be.

Sixteen-month-old Jimmy was extremely active for his tender age. It was hard to keep track of him. One day, he got into the kitchen, climbed up onto the table, and from there to the counter top from which he could reach into the cupboard. He took out a box of cookies, and by the time his mother came in and found him, he had eaten six of them and cookies were lying all over the place.

After that, he became even more troublesome. He climbed up onto anything and everything.

Punishing after the fact does not always prevent recurrence of the misbehavior. And it also has other disadvantages for both punished and punisher. To supervise is to prevent things from happening in the first place, before they can be enjoyed. And to *catch children when they are being good.*

Sylvia was reading a magazine on the front porch. Judy and Bill were playing in the back yard in the sandbox. For almost an hour, all was serene. The children's play was both quiet and cooperative. Then Bill grabbed a sand bucket that Judy was using and she tried to get it away from him. He resisted, and a fight ensued. When it had grown to drastic proportions, with Bill pulling Judy's hair and Judy kicking Bill's legs, and both of them screaming at the top of their lungs, Sylvia roused herself and went around the back to put a stop to the commotion. She was angry at having her reading interrupted and she was a little embarrassed in front of the neighbors. She took a child in each hand and proceeded to administer corporal punishment in the form of hard blows to each child's buttocks. She left them whimpering in their respective rooms and went back out on the porch.

Everyone knows that such scenes are common. Parents will protest in their own defense that they are people too and need time to themselves. But what are the effects of these measures on the children and on the parents? Do parents actually get the needed time to themselves through them? What parental behaviors would be more efficient and more pleasant for all concerned? Sylvia had paid no attention to her children during the long period in which things were going well. She used the time to take a needed rest for herself. Who can blame her? But her action did not decrease the chance that a similar incident will recur. It may even have made it more likely because of the emotionality of the situation and the bad feelings generated. Investigating other ways may be more beneficial.

Ruth was a former psychology student who was taking a couple of years off before completing her graduate work to be home with her two children, ages two and three. Because she was very aware of the principle of reinforcement, she took pains to see that desirable behavior in the children was rewarded. She tried to arrange things so that they were able to play within her sight at all times, and she used various means to remind herself to encourage such behaviors as cooperation, sharing play equipment, and "creativity," by which she meant anything from the construction of a block tower to filling play dishes with sand. When possible, Ruth stationed herself near where the children were playing. She tried to plan her day so that the tasks she engaged in while they played allowed her to monitor their activities.

If from this you get the idea that caring for children is a tough and demanding process, you've read me right. It requires a great deal of thought and some ingenuity too.

Lillian and Matthew's four-year-old daughter, Lyn, was the first grandchild on both sides of the family and she was the recipient of an endless stream of toys brought as gifts. Soon there were too many for the space available. Her parents considered giving or throwing some of the items away, but Lyn protested vehemently. There were also the feelings of the donors to consider.

The solution was suggested by a friend who was a behavioral psychologist. Whenever Lyn received a new toy, her parents surreptitiously removed one or more items in which she had shown little recent interest. These items were kept on a shelf in a closet. When Lillian or Matthew observed Lyn doing something they especially liked—anything from playing quietly while Lillian talked on the phone to behaving politely when her grandparents visited—they brought out one of the toys that she had not seen in several weeks. Lyn was delighted to see her new/old toy again.

If Lyn remembered and asked for a toy, it would be brought out on the next "catch-her-being-good" occasion.

The simple device of noticing and reacting positively when children behave well can have amazingly beneficial results. It is probably the single most important principle of child care. But it takes a real self-management program for most people because attention is more readily drawn to disruption of some sort.

When Bea realized that she was screaming at her children daily, she was determined to set the situation back on a positive course. Since she was an inveterate coffee drinker, she decided to let her impulse to have a cup of coffee be the cue. Before she got the coffee she would go to where the children were playing and if she saw them doing something she liked, she would praise them and chat for a minute or two.

Sylvia used a slightly different system. Each morning, she placed five poker chips in her pocket. By the end of the day she usually had managed to give them to her ten-year-old son, David, for coming right home from school, responding quickly when called, getting to his homework, practicing the piano, feeding the dog, general friendliness and cheerfulness, or anything else that she decided on. David did not know in advance just what action on his part would produce a poker chip. He liked to receive them because he could exchange them for a list of items on a "menu" that he and Sylvia had made up together. For example, with four chips he could "buy" ice cream, for ten he could get a model airplane, and for thirty he could go out to see a movie.

Try positive reinforcement. It really works.

One can also be creative in finding solutions to the problems raised by children.

Suzanne and Bernard had been married for five years and they really wanted children. But they were well aware of the problems that children would raise in their urban professional lives. Furthermore, when they took account of their income, their tastes, their joy in travel, they felt that the problems would be more than they wanted to take on if they had more than one child. On the other hand, they believed that it would not be in a child's best interests to grow up in a totally adult world.

Their attempted solution was not easy, but it was beautifully logical. They purchased a building containing six apartments and established a kind of communal arrangement with four other couples. One apartment was shared by all. It was used mainly for child care. Each of the couples had one child, but because of the living arrangements the children had playmates. Also, care of four children by eight adults allowed for rotating time off for the parents.

This very short discussion of some of the ways your self-management can help in the care of children is meant merely to suggest. Providing good care for children with a maximum of efficiency and a minimum of turmoil is very much a self-management matter. If you follow the principles we have discussed, you can achieve considerable control over the situation and much gratification. It takes some planning, some energy, and some ingenuity to make the most of any situation you analyze. But it's worth it.

Gnawings, Churnings, Itches and Tingles: Self-Managing Emotions

We can manage what we do, but what about how we feel? How do we manage ourselves when we are dragged down by a depression so severe that nothing seems worth it? How do we smile and deliver "reinforcement" when we are seething with anger? How do we pretend friendly indifference when we are burning with desire?

Psychologists believe that an emotion consists of a combination of our thoughts and our bodily state. Neither of these is under quite the degree of conscious control as are the muscles of our arm when we reach for a sip of coffee or of our legs when we go for a walk, or even our vocal apparatus when we speak. Our body state seems to be perceived fairly inexactly by us. The thoughts we are having and the situation we are in cause us to interpret the same body state differently on different occasions.

What do people usually do about their emotional condition? Of course, that depends partly on the emotion. They may simply enjoy it. They may want to kill, and sometimes people do kill under the impact of an emotion. They may attempt sexual seduction. They may prowl about the house looking vainly for relief. They may take substances designed to change their mood—alcohol, for example.

Emotions are states that drive us to action, but sometimes they are debilitating. Extreme depression, for example, is characterized by an overwhelming "what-does-it matter?" feeling. Even the slightest act may then be a horrendous chore requiring motivation and energy that just aren't there. Some depressions appear to be physiological in origin. Some seem to have a genetic basis. But others are clearly due to psychological conditions. Whatever its cause, extreme depression causes painful inactivity.

Can you self-manage yourself out of a depression? Or any other emotion, for that matter? The answer is a resounding yes. The techniques you use are much the same as those already discussed: For example, you coddle, plan, go in small steps, rearrange the environment to provide cues to changed behavior.

You begin by examining your situation. Discover the conditions that are associated with the undesirable emotional reaction. Often emotions depend on association. Something that has been present during an emotional state in the past evokes that state when it reappears. Actors wishing to cry real tears make use of this process by reminding themselves of something that makes them feel sad. They build up the mood by intensive imagining of the emotion-inducing associations. More often, we control our emotional reactions by not thinking about things that would induce a state of sadness, fear, or other unpleasant emotions. Sometimes we do this without realizing it; at other times, it is quite conscious.

More and more, behavioral psychologists who are in the business of helping people self-manage have begun to utilize their clients' imaginations as tools for the control of emotional states. The client is asked to vividly imagine a situation and then to imagine equally vividly either a pleasant or unpleasant consequence, depending on whether the imagined state is to be strengthened or weakened. The psychologists report that they have been successful in changing emotional states and desires through these methods.

Perhaps the best-known method in which imagining is used to control emotion is "systematic desensitization" for the control and reduction of fears. The client is asked to make a list of feared situations arranged in order from very fearful to slightly fearful, with gradations in between. She is also taught a system of relaxation. Relaxation, the proponents of this method say, is incompatible with fear. You cannot be both fearful and relaxed. After relaxation techniques have been learned, the behaviorist presents items from the list, beginning with the least fearful. The client concentrates on the item while maintaining the relaxation state. When there is success with the first item, the next item is presented and vividly imagined while relaxation continues—and so on up to the most feared items. Notice that our principles of coddling and small steps are involved.

Sometimes the counselor will help the client to arrange actual situations.

Sally was afraid of elevators and would not be able to accept a very desirable new job unless she was able to overcome the fear. She presented herself to a behavioral counselor for help. The consultant and Sally developed a list of situations. It went from "thinking about being in an elevator," the least frightening, up to "being in an elevator which got stuck between floors," the most frightening item on the list. In the consultant's office, Sally managed to remain calm and relaxed while imagining all items on the list.

She was then given "homework assignments." In the first, she stood in the lobby of the office building watching the people get on and off the elevators. She spent some time there every day for a week, gradually moving closer to the elevators as she was able to without feeling fear. Her counselor stressed that she must not push herself to try something for which she was not ready.

After Sally had accomplished feeling calm in the presence of elevators and of people getting off and on them, an arrangement was made with the elevator attendant so that Sally could stand inside a nonmoving elevator.

The first time Sally actually got on an elevator for a ride, she walked up to the first floor and took the elevator down one flight. Since she was less fearful when she was not alone in the elevator, it was arranged that a friend accompany her for these sessions. The gradual training was continued until Sally had completely lost her fear.

Notice that behavioral treatment methods tend to ignore the issue of how a person became fearful in the first place. Finding out how the reaction got started may sometimes help you change it; it also may take a lot of time and money, if you use psychotherapy to do so. And you may find that knowing the origin doesn't help at all. So these techniques are designed to work even without that. You self-manage your behavior, not your past. The behavior is what you can change.

The best way to control anger is a little more complicated than the time-honored practice of counting to ten. Avoid situations that induce anger at first. Then, gradually put yourself in situations that make you angry, so that control comes in small manageable steps. Work first in imagination. Only after you can remain calm while evoking a mental image of an anger-inducing situation should you allow yourself to try dealing with the real thing.

Gladys and Robert had been divorced for two years. During that time, they had developed even greater anger and bitterness than at the time of their separation. Gladys was unhappy about the financial arrangements and Robert was angry about the fact that he had been able to obtain permission to visit the children only on alternate weekends. Their relationship had cycled downward. The very sight of Robert's car in her driveway made Gladys angry and she usually managed to show how she felt. But it was wearing, and she decided that she would like to change the situation.

A friend recommended a behavioral counselor, who dealt with the situation much as fears are treated. First, Gladys constructed a list of the anger-inducing conditions. Then she learned to remain calm while imagining them in the office. Before trying to work in the real situation, she and the consultant role-played in the office. The counselor said things that Robert might say that would make Gladys angry, and Gladys gradually was able to remain calm and relaxed while playing her role.

In time, Gladys was no longer troubled by unpleasant emotional reactions to Robert's visits. Furthermore, she became more assertive in her relationship with him because she was no longer more concerned about trying to control her emotional reactions than about being able to deal realistically with the situation. She hired a new lawyer, who helped her obtain a more equitable financial settlement. No longer angry at Robert, she became more conciliatory with respect to the times he could visit the children.

The way to approach self-management of emotions is to view them as behavior like any other behavior. They are reactions to the environment and can therefore be controlled by controlling the environment and by gradually substituting for the troubling emotional response another reaction such as calm relaxation.

Another important aspect of controlling emotional responses is to attend to their associated bodily sensations. Where do you feel the emotion? Focus on the emotion *as a body sensation;* this will help you to pinpoint the situations that arouse it. It will also reduce the intensity of the discomfort surrounding the emotion, since focusing on body sensations takes your attention away from the thoughts accompanying the sensations. You may find yourself able to say, "Well, it's only a sensation, not even a pain, maybe just a very dull ache. I can live with that." Gradually, the emotion itself will recede.

The converse of reducing fears by pairing them with pleasant images is to *increase fear and anxiety about a situation by pairing its image with an imagined negative reaction.*

Evalyn, who was afraid of speaking in public, was scheduled to introduce the speaker at the next P.T.A. meeting. Every time she thought of the upcoming event, she also thought of how terrified she expected to feel. As the day approached, she found herself feeling worse and worse. With only ten days to go, she was so full of anxiety over the matter that she decided to plead conflicting duties and turn the task over to someone else.

Unwittingly, Evalyn had been training herself to be nervous whenever she evoked the image of speaking in public and paired it with anxiety. She might have done better by trying to push it out of her mind altogether. She *was* "making herself worse."

When we inhibit fantasizing about a loved one in an effort to overcome grief because the affair is breaking up; when we convert an emotion into a sensation; when we "go blank" in order to control urges to engage in acts we are trying to stop—in all these cases, we are exerting control rather than being the passive receptacles of uninhibited association of ideas. I was once asked if I didn't think that by suppressing thoughts of certain kinds we were not in danger of becoming more "mechanical" than "human." I said that managed and directed thinking, when it is we ourselves who are doing the managing and directing, seems not mechanical at all, but very human. I still don't know why anyone should think otherwise.

When you control your thoughts, you do so to further your selected aims, and for your greater comfort and pleasure. Whether a thought is undesirable or not depends on your goals. You decide what you want, and you can "change your mind" about it, too. We do not say that any kind of thinking is sinful or wrong, or even ill-advised, except in terms of its accordance with your own goals. We do say that with awareness of what certain kinds of thinking can lead to, you can direct your thinking toward the achievement of definite aims. Thinking is no longer only a clue to hidden intrapsychic processes; it is behavior like other behavior in that we can learn to control it in the interest of achieving our goals and of gaining greater contentment and happiness.

Sally, an experimental psychologist, allotted her first half-hour of wakefulness to what she called her "thinking agenda." Even before rising, and while she washed and brushed her teeth and made her morning coffee, she engaged in planned "thinking activities." She went over her research procedures and results in her mind to determine whether she had left out anything important in formulating the conclusions. By the time she sat down at her desk she was ready to begin.

Meditation is a form of thought control. In essence, it involves sitting comfortably in as quiet an atmosphere as one can find and focusing one's thoughts on a single object or scene or word. Other thoughts are gently brushed aside. The fact that this simple procedure is claimed to be highly beneficial—it is said, for example, to reduce oxygen intake, lower blood pressure, produce greater energy and attentiveness, induce sleep, and bring about a state of contented calm—indicates how potent directed thinking can be in affecting our emotional state and even our physical well-being.

Self-Managing Your Money

Too often, our buying impulses result from deliberate attempts to control our behavior by those whose financial gain depends on what we do. Hawkers are everywhere—on television and radio, on billboards, in the newspapers, in magazines, and on the shelves of shops and in the very packages in which the items we buy are wrapped. Every day, the mailbox contains messages from those who would control us in their own interest. Our credit card and utility bills come in envelopes stuffed with glossy pictures of items we might never have thought of purchasing, but which are seductively dangled before us. The hawkers try to catch us in weak moments—when we are tired, when our level is low. When we read the newspaper, our tired eyes stray from the small print of the news copy to the easy-to-read ads. Save 30¢ on a box of detergent, 12¢ on a pound of margarine! Travel now, pay later! The item you cannot afford to be without!

Of course, survival itself depends on having some degree of "sales resistance." An especially effective way to remain uninfluenced by the hawkers is to avoid their messages wherever possible. Train yourself not to look at the ads in the newspaper. Instead of magazines, read library books (which are free and which you select); turn off the TV altogether or get a remote-control device so you can remove the commercials from view and hearing. Throw out the ads that come in the mail without first browsing through them. Consult unbiased sources wherever possible to help with decisions about what products and brands are best. (*Consumer Reports* is an example of such an aid.)

You may find these suggestions a bit radical. And certainly, to follow them would mean quite a lot of change. But you can do so by using the self-management principles. First continue as usual, but notice how much time you spend paying attention to those who would manage you. Consider why you buy one item instead of another. This will indicate the extent of the influence you are under. Then plan to change. There are many things that can be done. Instead of looking through a magazine for ideas about what food to serve, look through a cookbook—look through a whole shelf of cookbooks. Instead of going to the supermarket with those little coupons in your fist, first make out your list, then use the coupons only for items which were on the list before you saw the ads for this week's "bargains." Instead of allowing yourself to be carried away by a fancy package, read the small print: the price, the quantity, and the ingredients. There are also books in the library that will help you develop stagies for shopping. Use the time you save avoiding ads to develop more systematic shopping methods.

I won't try to get into such things as growing your own herbs or vegetable garden except, again, to recommend the library for exploring such projects. But I would like to put in a plea that you look into the purchase of used items instead of new ones. Because most people have insufficient sales resistance, they often make purchases which overload them. A *House Beautiful* ad inspires the passionate need for wholesale redecorating. What happens to someone's old bed/refrigerator/couch/bureau/desk/chair/etc.? You get it at one-tenth its purchase price from a garage sale or an ad in the paper. Three dollars at the local thrift shop plus a little alteration easily done on Level Four time can produce a garment superior to what you would pay thirty dollars for if new.

Most of the well-known techniques for managing money are consistent with self-management principles. "Save a little every day" is the principle of small steps. Grocery lists help reduce impulse buying and prevent additional trips to the store for forgotten items. "Stay away from temptation" is another way of saying avoid antecedents to behavior you want to reduce. Find a substitute for the window shopping responsible for some of your heavier spending.

"Buy now, pay later" can be a disaster. Your capacity for making decisions about your life can be seriously affected when your entire income is earmarked for bills.

Then when a need comes up that cannot be delayed, like when your stove quits or your car insurance is due, you go further into debt. If ever planning is called for, it's in money matters—whether this means putting aside a little each week to replace the winter coat that has already seen three seasons since your rich aunt handed it down, or finding the spare cash for a trip to Paris. Only planning will bring about such long-range goals.

Self-Managing Work

Some of us "go to work." Some of us do "only housework." Some of us "work" better in the morning. Some have a "fifteen-hour workday." Some are "not working." Some "can't seem to get any work done." Some of us "love our work"; others "hate it."

Perhaps the theme that is most common to the "work" we speak of is that it produces a definite result and fits into a larger scheme, whether that be maintaining a household or conducting research on the DNA molecule. The activities which are not considered work tend to fall into the categories of caring for one's physical needs or entertainment. We do not consider eating, sex, elimination, or sleeping to be work. Nor do we generally consider watching television, playing tennis or chess, or reading a magazine to be work. Working is a means to a larger or other goal. Activities and functions which are ends in themselves are not considered work.

Often the goal of work is money. I work to put bread on the table to support my family. There is a real distinction made between work that is and work that is not paid for. When you are asked, "What do you do?", if you don't receive money as the specific result of the specific activities you perform, you might find yourself saying, "Nothing."

But let's assume that you are "employed" and do "real" work (for money). In that case, self-management may be of considerable help in improving various aspects of your work situation. The first step is to take stock of the situation you are in at present. For example, your capability-levels analysis may help you reorganize the tasks that you do on the job, provided you have a choice in such matters.

Suzy had always operated from a "first-things-first" conception in her job as clerical worker in an importing firm. The first thing she would do in the morning was to sort the mail. After her capability-levels analysis, that low-level job was moved to after lunch.

Even when you have no real choice, there may be some things you can do to improve the situation.

Polly was assigned to act as receptionist for the first three hours of the morning, a job that merely entailed announcing visitors, answering the telephone, and sorting the morning mail. Unfortunately, these fairly simple activities coincided with her high capability levels. She requested and was given additional filing to do, which pleased her boss and reduced her morning underemployment.

Oonagh had a similar problem which she solved by surreptitiously learning French vocabulary words between her other tasks.

Kate rearranged her daily schedule. Instead of getting up at 7:00 A.M. as she had formerly done, she laid out her clothes and breakfast the night before and by very skillful organizing was able to get up at 8:15 and still get to the office at 9:00 A.M. This reduced some of her early morning underemployment because it took her less than an hour to rise to the high level needed at the office.

Overemployment on the job may also call for re-scheduling.

Vera was an excellent stenographer in the afternoon, but only an average stenographer in the morning. She and Mildred, who had an opposite pattern, arranged things between them so that Mildred took dictation in the morning and Vera in the afternoon.

Being late to work (or any other place, for that matter) can be cured. The same principles apply here as to any other behavioral goal.

Bonnie chose being on time to work as her major behavioral goal. During baseline observation, she found that she was in the office by nine o'clock only twice during a two-week interval. The other days she was late from two to twenty minutes, with an average of seven and a half minutes a day.

Her first interim goal was to be no later than six minutes. For the next week, whenever she arrived six minutes after nine or earlier, she allowed herself of cup of coffee. During the first week she met her goal each day. The second week the criterion was changed to four minutes after nine. Within a month, she was never late anymore. The boss noticed and commented favorably.

If you are a boss, you can use a very similar technique with a chronically tardy employee.

Sybil kept a record of the time Angela, her assistant, arrived at the office during a two-week baseline period. The average lateness was eleven minutes. The following week, whenever Angela arrived earlier than that, Sybil arranged to greet her in a friendly manner. Sure enough, Sybil's greetings had an effect: Angela's new average was only six minutes. Six minutes late or earlier became the new criterion for a friendly greeting. In this way Sybil shaped Angela's behavior. After two months, Angela was no longer late.

Whether you are unemployed or looking for a better job, you can benefit from applying self-management methods to your job hunting. Many of us find looking for a job to be a very difficult and annoying problem. There are formidable application forms, letters to prospective employers, and, if you are serious (and you probably should be), the writing of an effective résumé. In other words, job hunting means writing, and writing, for most of us, requires top-level effort. All the self-management principles discussed earlier should be brought to bear on your job-hunting effort.

When Lindy decided to look for another job, she vowed that she would do everything within her power to increase her chances of success. She rose an hour early each morning and spent some high-level time working on the draft of her résumé. It took almost two weeks to finish, but it was worth it. She also drafted letters to prospective employers at that hour. In the evenings she typed her letters (a lower-level task when she was merely copying) and filled out "easy" parts of the applications she received.

Jobs are social situations. Skills in handling social problems can therefore be very important to your job performance. Again, refer back to the techniques that have been discussed. If you are spending too much time socializing, self-manage a reduction. If you feel you need to increase social interactions on the job, you can self-manage that too. But remember to begin with careful observation and analysis of the initial situation. That way you will be sure of the changes you want to make and will prevent yourself from taking on too much at once.

Self-Managing
with Others ...
and with Yourself

Remember how poor Robinson Crusoe suffered before Friday came along? He almost went totally mad from the frustration of not having another human being with whom to interact.

When we are in the presence of others, everything we do or fail to do, every facial expression, direction of gaze, and gesture affects those around us. When we smile, we strengthen the behavior of others that preceded our smile. If we express disgust with a grimace, we have a different effect. And just as our actions affect those around us, the actions of those around us influence *our* feelings and behavior. The reinforcing, nonreinforcing, and punishing effects exerted by others are pervasive and often quite subtle. We often are not aware of what aspects of our behavior are being affected.

If people are so affected by the subtle actions of those around them, and if we can control our own behavior, theoretically we can also learn to exert control over the reactions of others. In practice, like other aspects of self-management, it takes planning and deliberation.

Plus maybe a little bit more. We are all noodles in the social soup, affected by as well as affecting all the other noodles. Our behavior is largely under the control of the situation and our past experiences in similar situations. Social effects are so strong because of the great capacity we have for supplying effective behavioral consequences to one another. If you think about your life's goals, you will find that they are almost always dependent on others, or the actions of others: I want someday to win an Oscar or a Nobel Prize. I want to become an office manager. I'd like to succeed at my own small business. I want to make the baseball team. My goal is to write a great and successful novel. I want a home and children. I will find happiness if I can find someone to love who loves me. I'd like to be the life of the party. I want to be an opera star. All of these are socially reinforced behaviors; they require others.

Most often, our short-range goals are also social. We select our clothes, our forms of entertainment, our types of employment with some consideration of the social interactions that they will involve or produce. The shipwrecked survivor on an island all alone is regarded as undergoing a horrible trial. Solitary confinement is generally considered cruel. Yet simply having others around us is not enough to prevent loneliness. Interaction is also important. It was not just Friday's presence, but his response to Crusoe's behavior that reduced the loneliness. Such interaction—affecting the behavior of others and being affected in turn—makes a situation truly social.

Cycling

Most social relationships are unstable. Either they are getting better, or they are getting worse, or they are changing in intensity—or, put another way, the benefits the participants derive from them are changing. Even fifty-year-old good, solid partnerships—whether in business or marriage—alter over the years. And who has not had a friendship that once seemed full of promise but then floundered on misunderstandings and disappointments?

The reasons for cycling—both in an upward and downward direction—are not too difficult to understand. When one unpleasant thing happens, it is easier to find another one.

Linda and Marie had not known each other long, but already they seemed to be very good for each other. They enjoyed many of the same books and movies and both were excellent on the tennis court.

Then one day Marie waited over an hour and a half in a restaurant while Linda finished her shopping. She was terribly disappointed in her new friend, but she tried not to allow the incident to lead to a break between them. Linda apologized and promised that she would try never to keep Marie waiting again.

But now that one unpleasant incident had occurred between them, Marie began to notice other things about Linda that she found annoying—for example, the way Linda would sometimes change the subject of conversation just when Marie began to get interested in it, and the fact that their tastes in music were actually quite dissimilar.

When, about a month after the lateness incident, Linda failed to type up their minutes of the group meeting, as she had said she would, Marie exploded. The argument set them back still further, and Linda also began to participate in the cycle through increasingly negative expectations concerning Marie, who now appeared to her as rather grouchy and unreasonable.

To a great degree, expectations dictate perception. We observe what we are set to observe. This is why personal interactions involve cycling in both directions.

Sometimes something happens that runs counter to our expectations and that reverses the cycle.

Because he had been in military service during most of her babyhood, Mitchell had never felt very close to his five-year-old daughter, Jan. And obviously Jan was shy and uncomfortable in her father's presence, often clinging to her mother and refusing to sit on Mitchell's lap. After a while, since he had come to expect rejection from his little girl, Mitchell began to avoid her and to focus more of his attention on Peter, his three-year-old son, a strategy which only made matters worse. Then one afternoon when Jan and Mitchell were alone together in the house for several hours while his mother took Peter to the pediatrician, an event occurred which set up a positive cycle between Jan and her father.

At first, they more or less ignored each other. Mitchell was reorganizing his phonograph record collection in the living room and Jan was playing with crayons at the kitchen table. After a while, Mitchell came into the kitchen to get some materials for cleaning the stereo cabinet. Jan had just finished a rather creditable rendition of a house and tree. For her age, it was truly a remarkable production, and her father, who had done a term project on children's drawings in college, was aware of it.

"Jan, that's a really good picture," he said. "May I have it to put on my wall at the office?"

Jan was very pleased and beamed at him as she handed him the drawing. This little incident initiated new and positive expectations on both their parts. Mitchell began to find other things about his daughter to admire, and Jan lost her shyness. A few weeks later Jan had begun to run to her father when he came home in the evening, as Peter did but as she had never done before.

Changes in relationships are constantly occurring as positive and negative incidents occur; as interests drift from one thing to another and behaviors change; as other relationships wax or wane, either taking up more time or leaving more time free; or as changes in job or residence occur. It is helpful to be alert to these changes. Notice the beginning of a downward trend.

You can sometimes help to change its direction and initiate a positive cycle. It can be a serious mistake to focus on areas in which problems exist; they may then only become more glaring.

Assessing Relationships

Friendships and other relationships with people are important in our lives. They are also time-consuming. There is a limit to how much we may wish to invest in any given relationship in view of what we receive from it. It may seem cold and heartless to think of evaluating people this way, but we must of necessity make some choices and selections. Many of us spend too much of our time with others. Sometimes we simply don't know how to get out of doing so.

Carol decided that her life needed a lot of reorganizing. She was finding it very hard to get her work done. Something or someone always seemed to interrupt.

She made a list of all those with whom she interacted more or less regularly. Over the next month, she recorded every interaction, noting the time of day it occurred, her capacity level at the time, the type of interaction (meeting in a public place, alone or in a group, at whose house, by telephone, etc.), the nature of the activities engaged in and/or topics discussed, and an assessment of the value of the exchange in Carol's subjective viewpoint.

At the end of the month, Carol analyzed the information she had collected. The sources of her dissatisfaction were obvious. Martha, her upstairs neighbor, turned out to be a frequent visitor who popped in for some trivial reason three to four times a week. Martha's visits often caused Carol to lose time from her work. She also noted that Brenda, an acquaintance of many years, was a person she really enjoyed being with, but that somehow they met only very rarely.

Having pinpointed some of the problems, Carol had little trouble making adjustments. Martha was understanding when Carol explained that she needed her high levels for work. They began to have lunch-time visits that were planned in advance. Brenda, who was passive about social situations herself, was delighted when Carol called and suggested they get together to go bicycle riding on Sunday afternoon.

Being deliberate about social relationships is uncommon in this society. It almost seems as if there is an unwritten rule that social interactions should be spontaneous and unrehearsed. But busy people find that social relationships are no less important than business or professional relationships and interactions. They can be more or less enjoyable, more or less rewarding, more or less *efficient.*

Lucy and Miriam were former roommates who now lived in cities several hundred miles apart. Their time together was very limited, to their mutual regret. Both microbiologists, they had professional as well as personal interests in common.

Not only did they see each other too infrequently these days, but Lucy noticed that the little time they did have together was not as well utilized as it might have been. The last time Miriam came for the weekend, they had gone to a movie on Friday night, had spent Saturday morning discussing how Lucy should redecorate her living room (Miriam, Lucy believed, had excellent taste in such matters), had shopped for groceries on Saturday afternoon, and cooked dinner for some mutual friends Saturday evening. The friends did not leave until almost three o'clock in the morning, and Sunday there was hardly time for brunch before Miriam had to leave for the airport.

Lucy was very dissatisfied. In their letters to one another they had discussed some of the research problems they were having and had planned to talk further about those things during the weekend of Miriam's visit. As it had turned out, the conversation had not once turned to microbiology.

Lucy reviewed the weekend's activities. Going to the movies

together was simply silly. There was no need to spend their precious time together doing something they could do equally well individually. On Saturday morning they had wasted their Levels One and Two on personal things because (1) they had made no plan to do otherwise and (2) they had not had any time to talk before then because of the movie. An even bigger mistake was having company for dinner Saturday night. They spent too much time preparing the meal and the evening shared with others was too long.

Lucy wrote out her analysis and suggestions in a letter to Miriam. Miriam responded with wholehearted agreement. Their next weekend was spent very differently, to the greater mutual pleasure and benefit of both women.

In this case, it was not the relationship itself that needed change, but the activities which Lucy and Miriam engaged in when they were together. They simply needed more of a different kind of time together. They needed more time when both were at the capability levels needed to discuss their mutual professional interests.

Often problems that appear to be problems in the relationship between two people are really problems with the activities engaged in or problems with the levels at which people are interacting.

Bea's mother had a habit of stopping by to visit her daughter in the morning as she returned from shopping. At first, Bea enjoyed the morning visits, but after a while they became more and more difficult to endure. Bea felt the relationship deteriorating. She did not want to hurt the older woman, who was getting on in years and had already lost some of her dearest friends. Still, Bea shuddered at the thought that the visits which she found so terribly boring would probably not stop unless she found a way to stop them.

The solution to Bea's problem came through her capability levels analysis. The older woman's talk of mundane affairs produced feelings of extreme underemployment in Bea. Although she had already tried to sew and do light chores during the visits, those activities were insufficient to lift the activity so that it fitted her level. Bea tactfully explained to her mother that she was going to schedule her work period for mornings and hoped that her mother could visit in the afternoon when she would be freer to talk.

The new arrangement worked well. The two women would have a cup of tea together on the porch when it was warm enough and Bea would knit while her mother talked. At that hour of the day, Bea was rarely impatient, argumentative, or even bored.

Sometimes two people differ greatly in interests and ability levels but can still have a good relationship if they interact at times when they are at their most compatible. Without realizing it, some people bring down their level through alcohol to be at a level compatible with those around them. Alcohol also diminishes anxiety in some users, and its effects differ somewhat (sometimes greatly) from one person to the next. But it is the great "leveler" at parties; it is what keeps many people from being bored.

As you examine the various relationships you have with your friends and acquaintances, consider the possibility of improving them by (1) reducing or increasing the time spent together, (2) having the time together occur at a different capability level, or (3) changing the type of activities in which you engage when together.

In addition to their afternoon visits, Bea and her mother occasionally went to auctions together. Their shared pleasure during these days contributed further to their fondness for each other. Bea looked back on those dreadful days of morning visits with amazement.

When two individuals are both aware of their levels, it becomes possible for them to communicate with one another about them in order to find the best times for interacting.

Sheri rose in the middle of the night in order to complete her daily stint of work before the rest of the world got out of bed. Of course, this meant that she was out of phase with her son, Floyd. She was even more out of phase with him than with others because he also kept unusual hours—in the other direction. He worked at night and slept until noon. Although there was no way to really solve the problem, at least they both recognized it and did not blame each other for the difficulties they had while one was at Level One and the other at Level Five.

When a relationship seems unsatisfactory in some way, begin by analyzing activities jointly engaged in and the levels at which interactions between you and the other person are taking place. Downward cycling can often be halted by the simple expedient of rescheduling.

Unbalanced Relationships

It is also possible that the relationship which has begun to trouble you has become unbalanced. This happens when the returns to one individual continue, or even increase, but lessen for the other. Because relationships often drift away from what they were initially, continued reappraisal is important. When one person expects from another something that is not forthcoming, disappointment is inevitable. It can be very hard to be realistic about the situation.

Unbalanced relationships, in which one individual derives more satisfaction from the relationship than the other, can be very stable, if stability is measured by duration.

Grace and George had been married for twenty years. Grace always felt that she was giving much more to the relationship than she was receiving. George would also admit that this was probably true. Grace met his needs for a wife, but his work often kept him away from home, and his wandering eye often gave him pleasures elsewhere as well. Yet their marriage endured and there were few open disagreements. To most people, it seemed a good marriage.

It is probably the rare relationship that is perfectly balanced, but it may be well to examine your current relationships for imbalance of an extreme or particularly unsatisfactory sort. Remember that it is the satisfaction or lack of satisfaction actually derived by which the relationship should be assessed. A relationship that may seem imbalanced to others may be quite satisfactory to those directly involved:

Jim did all of Marion's gardening on her two-acre lot. He also painted her house without charge. To others, theirs seemed an unbalanced relationship in which Jim was getting the short end of the stick. But that was not how Jim looked at it. Marion was tutoring him in French and mathematics. Although she spent less time tutoring than he did in caring for her property, the value of her instruction was great. He was very happy with the arrangement and consequently quite generous with his time.

Not that exploitation in relationships does not occur. It does.

Lori was in love with Spencer. She provided him with sexual partnership, cleaned his apartment, mended his clothes, listened to his complaints about his co-workers, and cooked most of his meals. He gave her the pleasure of his company and once in a while took her to a movie or to dinner. He was careful to show enough interest in her to keep her from leaving. On several occasions, when she announced that she was fed up and would not see him again, he declared his affection and promised to change. Lori was unhappy, but in her state she wished only that Spencer would show more concern for her and appreciation of the things she did.

Exploitation occurs when what one person can give is so needed by the other that the latter is willing to give more than a fair share in return. This is the kind of imbalance that makes for a very unhappy situation. Since being in love is an emotion, the only solution is for the exploited person to handle her reaction through self-management.

There is a word used to describe the kind of relationship in which both members get value commensurate with what they contribute to the relationship: "symbiosis." In symbiotic relationships, everybody profits.

But many relationships are not mutually gratifying, or do not seem to be even when they really are. The problems seem to be due to a law of human interaction that I have called the Law of Giving and Taking: *What is given seems larger to the giver than it does to the recipient.* This law poses great difficulties in human relationships.

When Donna looked back over the five years that she and Lynne had been friends, she recalled the many favors she had done for Lynne—taking care of her dog while she was on vacation, going to the hospital to visit every day after her operation three years ago, lending her countless books (some of which were not returned), listening for hours to her problems with her lover, or helping her to decide whether to quit her job.

Of course, Lynne had been a good friend, too. Donna does not like to think of what would have happened to her without Lynne when her mother was ill last year and Lynne helped in everything from getting the plane tickets to calling Donna's boss to explain why she would not be in for a few days. And there were other things, too. But now that she and Lynne were having troubles in their relationship, it seemed to Donna that on balance it had been she who had contributed more and received less from the relationship.

In Lynne's view, unsurprisingly, it was not Donna, but she who had given more.

Often the problem is not simply bias or misperception, but true lack of information.

Susan really resented it when Jill asked her to pick up some groceries, although she never told Jill how she felt about it. The problem was that the only store open after work was several blocks out of her way, a real inconvenience after she had been on her feet all day at the job. Jill truly did not realize how inconvenienced Susan was by her request. If she had, she would never have asked her to do it.

That kind of situation spells eventual trouble for the persons involved, and it also suggests something that might reduce the intensity of the problem. Susan might have done well to indicate that getting groceries after work was difficult instead of doing it and resenting it. Why do people often do things they do not want to do or which are really a nuisance? Often, they do them for the short-run gain of avoiding a slightly unpleasant situation or of doing a favor. Many of us have difficulty refusing a request. "No" can be one of the hardest words to say. When you analyze your relationships with others, consider the possibility that what seems like symbiosis to you might seem like exploitation to the other person, and, conversely, give heed to the possibility that you are becoming resentful over favors you are actually doing through sheer passivity or mistaken expectations.

In truth, the reason Mary was angry over what she had done for Paul was not because he had asked her to do it or even expected it, but because she had done it hoping he would return the favor. When it finally became clear that he would not, she felt she had been "used" and was really angry at herself for being a fool.

Mary's situation suggests another law: *Whenever you are angry at someone, you are probably even more angry at yourself.* Keep it in mind; you might find it helpful.

Behavior in Groups

So far in this chapter on social interactions, I have concentrated on two-person interrelationships and interactions. But much of our behavior takes place in larger groups—as when four or five colleagues have lunch together, when you spend an evening with a dozen dinner guests, or you attend a local schoolboard meeting of a hundred persons or more. Some people find that the larger group situations pose special problems for them.

The smaller groups have some interesting characteristics which it may be valuable for you to consider. The three-person group, for example, is unstable. At any moment it can be seen to be functioning as a two-one interaction. Rarely is it actually three equal and independent persons. Any mother of three can bear me out on that.

Lucy, Anne, and Flora—ages five, six, and eight respectively—spent most of their time together because the family lived in a remote rural area where the nearest other child was too far away to walk to every day.

By most standards, the three sisters got along quite well except that there always seemed to be a certain "ganging up" of two against one. Usually it was Anne and Flora who would lead in imaginative play. Although Flora was older, Anne usually had the ideas that were used. This left Lucy. For example, Anne and Flora would make themselves competing rulers of neighboring monarchies and Lucy would be assigned the job of messenger. Or Anne and Flora would be parents, Lucy their child.

Less often, the two younger girls would pair off in some physical activity such as rolling down the front lawn or picking flowers.

Even in conversations among adults, the three-person group can be seen as having a fluctuating characteristic.

Martha usually spent one or two evenings with Corinne and Alison, who shared an apartment. Depending on the topic, it seemed that there were always two persons holding one view with the third holding a slightly different view. Martha and Corinne might have enjoyed a certain book, but Alison either didn't like it or had not read it. Martha and Alison, on the other hand, shared an interest in indoor gardening which Corinne did not share. And so it went. Not that it was a problem. In fact, on many things the three friends tended to agree. But Martha noticed the two-one split tendency was very often there, even when only slightly or subtly.

The two-one split among three persons also occurs within larger groups. In the four-person group, sometimes you get a two-two split, less often a three-one split or a two-one-one split. These splits may not be actual disagreements, but merely varying intensities of interest in particular subjects.

The nature of a discussion and the topics that come up for discussion depend on the number of people in the group, especially the number of active participants, since there will often be completely silent witnesses in any but the smallest-size group. In a group of seven, for example, only three or four of the persons present may be vocal.

In informal groups, the range of topics and the way they are dealt with change drastically as the size of the group increases. In general, the larger the informal social group, the narrower the range of possible topics and the more superficially they are handled. This should not be at all surprising. The successful group discussion is one that includes all who are present, but the more people with varying interests there are, the fewer the areas of common interest will be. Usually, one tries to keep disagreements in such groups to a minimum, so controversial topics (politics and religion) are omitted.

Other things being equal, possibly the largest or most noticeable change comes as one goes from the two-person to the three-person group. Evaluate the types of group interactions in which you participate with all these ideas in mind. We often find that social pressures bring us into group situations that we later wish we had avoided. Even if they were not terribly unpleasant, they were time-wasters because we were not really interested in the discussion.

At a professional conference, Sybil wanted to talk to people whom she had not seen in a year or in several years because she had certain specific things she wanted to discuss. The first evening she had dinner with five women, all of whom were in that category. But the group discussion did not permit getting down to the more serious topics that she wanted to explore. She therefore made one-to-one appointments with several of them and was truly amazed at how efficiently she was able to get to the things that were important to her.

When Sonia went out West on vacation to visit relatives, she usually found that at each place she stopped there would be a whole group of people—aunts, cousins, and their children—that had turned out to visit with her. It was fun and it was also exhausting. Somewhat frustrating, too, because with so many people around, there was little chance to focus on individuals. One day, in Denver, at the home of a relative she had met only once before many years ago, she found herself having a long, leisurely talk with one of her second cousins. She was pleased at how interesting the conversation was and at how much she learned about that one person. They also found they had many common interests.

Think about your social relationships in terms of the size of the groups in which you customarily interact. When two persons have little in common or disagree on many topics but for some reason feel obliged to maintain a relationship with one another, it can be more comfortable for them to interact only when others are present. The superficiality of the conversation then seems less forced and the focus can be on the others present. Also, some people are distinctly uncomfortable when the discussion gets serious and therefore avoid two-person interactions. People who seem to prefer to interact with you only when others are around may be trying to avoid the intimacy and/or intensity of two-person interaction.

Then there are those who enjoy playing to an audience—the larger the better. The "life of the party" could scarcely sing songs or tell jokes with the same effect to an audience of one or two. Larger groups close off some types of behavior, but they do permit others. I recommend only a bit of cool analysis so that you can evaluate the groups you interact with in terms of how they meet both your short- and long-range goals.

Finding Your Group

Aside from particular friends and acquaintances, you probably interact with one or more groups. These may consist of members of your church or social set, neighbors, school friends, colleagues, relatives, or others. You probably find that you feel more comfortable with some of these groups than you do with others. The members of some of them are more similar to you with regard to fundamental values than is the case in other groups. In some of the groups you might even feel uncomfortable, alien. Perhaps you are not particularly fond of its members; they might not like you, either. And this can make you feel as if there were something wrong with you—when it's just that you are in the wrong group.

Ginny always felt like she did not belong. The feeling had started in high school and continued through her first year in college. In her second year, she joined the Music Club and her life was transformed. Instead of trying to adjust her behavior to people who were not interested in the things she liked, she suddenly found herself respected and approved of for the very things she had previously been rejected for: her intense involvement with music.

Arlene would bring a book with her to the playground, but she began to feel that the other women there resented her reading. But their conversations about the routine occurrences in a homemaker's day or about what had happened with so-and-so who had been having difficulties in her marriage didn't interest her. Nevertheless, she did not discontinue her reading, and whenever she felt that she could, she would contribute her own constructive thoughts, mentioning that she had read about a similar situation in one of her books.

Some of the women continued to resent her, but by taking this approach she discovered a small group who were interested in the subject matter she was reading and who even asked her for the titles of books she had read. Ultimately she began a book-exchange club among this group.

This last example demonstrates that sometimes the group itself might change through your efforts.

Don't let failure to fit in with a particular group undermine your feelings about your ability to interact with others. Instead, look for other groups and new acquaintances.

Reinforcing Others for Reinforcing You

The best kind of social situation is one in which the participants are mutually reinforcing, in which desirable behaviors are strengthened through the interaction. You can help produce this situation through deliberate action.

Marie felt that her marriage was going down the drain and little could save it. Ned, her husband, had become sullen and unresponsive. He never showed any gratitude for what she did for him or concern for her feelings. Marie felt very unhappy about the situation and sought help from a behavioral counselor.

For the first two weeks, she was asked to observe Ned's behavior toward her carefully. To Marie's surprise, she found that once in a while he did do something positive. She had been overlooking the "rare occasions." The counselor pointed out that these were the behaviors that must be built up. When Ned said or did something nice, Marie was to suppress her impulse to say, "Well, it's about time," and instead smile or say thank you. When Ned did something unpleasant, she was to ignore it as much as possible.

There is no question but that we can influence the way others behave toward us by how we react to their behavior. To increase actions that please us, we should arrange for them to be rewarded.

Making Assumptions

The law of parsimony, according to scientists, refers to a principle of analysis. According to this principle,

one should accept the simplest explanation of something, the one that calls on the smallest number of unusual and inexplicable events, at least as a first guess,
rather than invent a fancy and elaborate interpretation
drawing on many unknowns and unknowables.

An example of not obeying the law of parsimony occurs when anxious parents find their teen-ager still out
at two in the morning and assume death by auto accident. Not that auto accidents do not occur. They do.
And they are more likely to happen to persons of that
age and at that time of night. But they are far less likely
to be the cause of lateness than a party still in full swing,
peer pressure to stay out longer, "forgetfulness," car
trouble such as a flat tire—or, if an accident, a minor
one that produces delay but no injury. The statistics of
common causes for teen-age lateness don't support the
parent's immediate conclusion.

So it is advisable to do little interpretation, especially
of a negative sort. The opposite of adhering to the law
of parsimony is called paranoia. I'm not talking about
the mental illness, but of the way the term is used in
everyday language. You are being paranoid when you
accept more negative and complicated explanations
than the available evidence warrants. Sometimes,
though, after reviewing all reasonable explanations
first, you find that suspicions are warranted.

When Beryl was passed over for promotion, she tried to analyze
the situation as objectively as possible. She considered her length
of tenure at the job and compared her initial qualifications with
those of others who had received the promotion that she had
been denied. On every count, she should have been promoted.
Nor had she received any hint that there was something remiss
about her performance. She decided that she was the victim of
sex discrimination. The office of human rights agreed with her
and she initiated a legal action. Although it took two years, she
won the promotion as well as retroactive back pay.

Friendly Assumptions

Related to the concept of parsimony is a tactic I call "friendly assumptions."

When Madge did not show up for what Jeanne had believed was a firm lunch date, she decided that most probably Madge had forgotten because Jeanne had not been clear enough. She did not assume that *really* Madge did not want to lunch with her. If that were true, Jeanne would find out in time. There would be a clear pattern. It was not a conclusion which she would make on the basis of one missed appointment.

To make friendly assumptions instead of unfriendly ones is a kind of loyalty. You assume the best. Not that sufficient evidence could not convince you otherwise, but you will not jump to the unfriendly conclusion. That this makes very good sense can be demonstrated by imagining you are wrong. If you are wrong in your friendly assumption, your friendliness may in itself clear up whatever the problem was. If not, is very much lost? On the other hand, if you assume the worst, you may have initiated the downward spiral that will cost you a friend. And a friend lost is a loss indeed.

When Bernie did not call on Saturday as he had promised, nor on Sunday or Monday either, Myra considered the possibility that he was getting tired of their relationship, had found someone new, or was even angry at her for some unknown reason. But she adopted the friendly-assumption strategy. On Tuesday, she wanted to talk to Bernie about something she was working on (they worked for the same company). She not only brought herself to make the call, but to do it with an attitude of friendliness, in the belief that whatever had kept him from calling was trivial and not an indication in itself that their relationship was going inevitably downhill.

Bernie was very happy and relieved at Myra's call. He had

worked all day Saturday on the magazine article he had been trying to finish for months. Likewise on Sunday—and Monday he was kept late at the office. He had begun to feel guilty about not calling and was delighted when Myra called him.

It is not always easy to make friendly assumptions. Sometimes acting up at the first sign of trouble might even be a better tactic. But rarely. Statistics are on the side of imagining the best, not the worst. The paranoid person ends up alone with those worst imaginings coming true as people get tired of hearing tales of endless suspicions. And the moral of that is: Even if you feel upset over what seems to be a slight, try to keep your feelings at bay long enough to give the other person a chance to come around. Sometimes negative feelings are quite transient.

Being friendly to someone to whom your feelings are not friendly may be so difficult that you may need to set up a plan for going about it step by step.

Think of all those persons with whom you come into regular contact and about whom you have negative feelings which you wish you could manage not to show. Arrange a hierarchy starting from the person toward whom you would have the least difficulty being friendly, down to the person with whom there would be the next-least difficulty, and so on, all the way down to your absolute enemy (if you have one) whom you would rather either cut coldly or just sound off at. Then begin with the easiest ones. Deliberately seek these people out and say a few friendly things. Just be careful that you dispense your friendliness *contingently*. In other words, after you have selected the persons you want to receive your friendly attention, wait until they are doing something that you like. They may be smiling at you, saying hello, or even being helpful to someone else. It is particularly important not to dispense your friendliness immediately following some negative behavior on their part—for example, scowling. If you do, and your behavior is reinforcing, you might strengthen their negative behavior.

Observation and Analysis

Aspects of your social interaction that you want to improve or change will require the same principles and approaches we have discussed in previous chapters.

As you go through your normal everyday activities, be observant. Take notes. Decide on goals and on a step-by-small-step method of approaching those goals.

Phyllis said that she felt one of her greatest problems in social situations was her tendency to go along with anything that others asked of her or anything that they suggested.

Her self-management consultant suggested that she make careful observations over a two-week interval and then return for discussion and further planning. Phyllis carried a small notebook with her and wrote down the following whenever a social interaction that either pleased or displeased her occurred: date, time, other persons involved, what they did, what she did, and why she felt it was an example of a pleasing or not pleasing interaction.

When she returned to the consultant, they went over her notes together. These notes formed the basis of further action.

Ginger felt very awkward in social situations. She was extremely nervous, even in two-person interactions, and when there was more than one person with her, she almost fell to pieces or, rather, to near total silence. She felt that when she did speak she was unable to express herself well.

Her self-management project began with an examination of current behavior. For two weeks, she carried a small tape recorder with her and recorded herself during interactions with others. When she played back the tape, she found that her efforts at participation in social situations were not as fumbling as she had imagined. Her confidence was therefore increased, and this in turn led to even more successful interactions.

Mildred carried a small notebook with her which she had handy whenever a social interaction occurred on campus. She was a dramatics student and shyness was no problem, but her ambition was to be a comedian and she practiced on those around her. She noted down in her book whenever the person she was talking to responded by laughing. And she plotted the proportion of times she evoked laughter for each day.

Listening back to yourself on a tape can sometimes undermine your confidence. It depends on what your expectations are. Ginger's image of herself in social situations was so disparaging that just hearing herself emit sentences was a boost.

The tape recorder is very good for rehearsal.

Ginger later used her tape recorder for training. First, she wrote some questions and comments that might occur in ordinary conversation, and then she read them into the recorder leaving a blank space for her reply. For example:

"Hello, Ginger, How are you?"

Blank space.

"That's nice to hear. What did you think of that movie we saw last night?"

Blank space.

When she played back the tape, Ginger had to supply the answers. At a still later stage, Ginger also recorded her comments so that she could analyze them.

It is truly amazing what one can hear—and be able to correct or improve—through the use of the tape recorder. To get a real situation that does not involve the ethically questionable use of a hidden recorder, tape-record just your end of telephone conversations. When you listen back, look for the good things and concentrate on building those up. If you focus on your mistakes, the procedure might backfire altogether.

In analyzing your own social behavior, recognize the importance of planning. Most self-management comes from planting some kind of cue or antecedent so that you will be reminded to engage in more desirable actions. More than any other type of situation, social situations are distracting. It is literally hard to remember what you had hoped to change about your own behavior.

Kathryn felt that her major social problem was not being friendly enough. At night, as she was going to sleep, she often recalled the day's events and vowed that the next day she would be more friendly toward others. But when the next day came, she found that in the "heat" of the situations, she would forget and behave in the same old way. She had to be more deliberate about it, she decided. She carried around an index card, and for each social interaction she noted whether she had remembered her plan. The knowledge that she was keeping records seemed to act as a cue in itself. Her forgetfulness gradually ceased.

Cindy's problem was that she talked too long on the telephone. She was too friendly. She placed a notebook and stopwatch by the telephone and placed a cardboard box over it. On the box, she had written in large letters: SET THE TIMER. Because she had to lift the box to pick up the phone, she did not forget to time her calls. After each call, she recorded the person she had spoken to, whether it was she or the other person who had placed the call, and the duration of the conversation. The length of her telephone conversations went down dramatically. She was very pleased.

Next, she removed the box and found that she still remembered to set the timer. Still later, she stopped timing and recording, but she felt she had learned how to have shorter phone conversations and that it was no longer a problem.

Cues should always be removed as soon as you can do without them. That way, the behavior is on its own. But don't hesitate to introduce reminders again if they are needed.

Learning by Watching Others

Some people seem closed, unreadable. You feel that you don't know what they are thinking and you find it hard to predict what they will do. Others are accessible, open, and easy to relate to. We are probably all shy in some situations, but the behavior of open people helps reduce the fear and uncertainty that we might otherwise feel. They make us comfortable. If we want to cause that same reaction in others, watching the behavior of those who cause it in us will provide a model after which to pattern our own actions.

Similarly, if we want to learn to be more effective in certain situations, we can look for those who seem always to manage to pull off a power play, or get themselves in the favored position at a gathering—both geographically and psychologically. Watch them carefully. What, exactly, do they do? Do they seem open while actually revealing little? Notice how they manage this. Are they self-assured and assertive? What specific actions on their part communicate self-assurance and assertion?

After picking up new social skills by watching others, the next step is to role-play in your imagination, like the worker practicing in front of the mirror before asking the boss for a raise. The advantage of rehearsing is that you can control the intensity of your reactions and ensure progress in small steps; tackling real situations may plunge you in too deep, too soon. Later, when you begin to try out new social behaviors in real situations, you will have had some practice.

Nonverbal Behavior

It has been estimated that far more communication takes place at a nonverbal than at a verbal level. We send nonverbal, often unconscious, messages through our posture, clothing, gestures, nearness and distance from others, and, most importantly, through our eye movements. Within the last twenty years, psychologists have begun to study these things, and there are a number of books about this area of research that you can read. You will find that it is helpful to be aware of the nonverbal messages reaching you and of those you send.

For example, notice how close or how far from you other people stand or sit. In which direction are their bodies oriented: toward or away from you? Most people give nonverbal indications when they are bored such as drumming with their fingers, looking around at other people or out the window, or, yes, the old familiar yawning. Notice that behaviors that communicate boredom are exactly those which the etiquette books advise us to avoid.

Do people get closer to you than you would consider appropriate to the situation and to your relationship? If so, are they deaf, do they come from a culture in which persons customarily assume closer positions to the person they are speaking with than you are used to—or are they being sexually seductive? Eye contact is both subtle and powerful. If some people make you uncomfortable, or if you feel that they are being more intimate in their manner than you would have expected, your feeling may result from their eye movements.

Being late, not keeping an appointment, writing a short or long letter, bringing or not bringing a gift, insisting or not insisting on paying the check or your part of it—all of these are behaviors to which others will respond. The importance of this subject should not be judged by the small amount of space devoted to it here.

It is especially helpful to be able to recognize when verbal and nonverbal messages from a given individual do not seem to coincide. On the other hand, resist too much interpretation of such behavior. Sometimes the reasons are more benign than they appear. It is unreasonable to interpret all lateness as an expression of hostility. It may seem that way if you are the one who is being kept waiting on a street corner, but trains do arrive late, alarm clocks do fail, and taxis are sometimes hard to find. The person who is *always* late is something else, however, no matter how seemingly reasonable each excuse is.

Shyness

If you are shy, it means that your appropriate response has been inhibited by fear. Probably there are situations that provoke shyness in everybody, even the most outgoing persons. Some people are shy before groups of certain sizes. Usually larger groups are more likely to evoke shyness, but some people fear smaller groups. Successful stand-up comedians in nightclubs might appear to be the least shy people, but visit them a few minutes later in their dressing room and you might get a very different picture.

In analyzing your own shyness, think in terms of specific situations. At home, alone, playing with your dog, you may be the least shy. You may engage in behaviors under those circumstances that you would inhibit in most, if not all, other situations. You might be most shy in class, while shopping, when interviewed for a job, or while with your lover. Or any of these may be just the situations in which you are not shy at all. While shyness may sometimes seem charming, it can also be a great burden. It means that because of fearfulness, anxiety, or nervousness you fail to do what is best for you, and for your long-range happiness.

Shy people seem unlucky; their worst fears often come true. The result is an increase in fear and even more shyness.

One of the worst things about shyness is that it often looks like something else. When a shy person averts her glance to avoid a greeting, the person snubbed is more likely to attribute the action to lack of concern, snobbishness, unfriendliness, and disinterest than to fearfulness. People are often quite hostile to the person who is shy in their presence. And shy people often mask their nervousness with gruffness. On the inside, shyness may be friendliness and concern inhibited by nervousness; on the outside it may appear as crude impoliteness.

To cure yourself of shyness, use the principles we have already discussed. First observe yourself in various situations and try to discover both the antecedents (situations that produce the shyness reaction) and consequents (things that seem to keep shyness going). Then arrange the situations in order from those that produce least shyness to those that produce the most. Next, work in your imagination with the situations that produce least shyness. When you can imagine yourself engaging in the appropriate behavior without anxiety in those situations, go on to imagine other, more fear-inducing, situations. When you can handle them in imagination, then do some "fieldwork." You might follow some of the suggestions made in the section on assertiveness training a little further on in this chapter. Note also those situations in which you are not shy. Try to transfer the feelings you have in them to the situations you are fearful of.

Do not think of yourself as a shy person, but rather as someone who is shy in some circumstances and is going to train herself to be less so. By recognizing in advance the kind of situations that produce a shyness reaction, you will be more likely to prepare yourself in advance.

Learn to be able to say to yourself, "The situation I am entering now is one in which I have in the past been shy. I will be relaxed and will look for an opportunity to reduce my shyness by behaving appropriately although not by taking on too much at once, either."

Winifred was shy with men. Her shyness had caused her a lot of pain and trouble. She also tended to have no say in what she and her date did when they went out. When the man asked her what she would like to do, she almost always simply turned the question back to him.

In her retraining program, Winifred began by preparing herself mentally for a date with someone she knew fairly well and with whom she was less shy than with others. Before the date, she concentrated in her imagination so that she would not "forget" her good intentions. Also, she planned to confine herself to just two things: She would mention an activity—she decided on bowling—and she would insist on getting home by eleven-thirty.

The result was successful. Not only did she enjoy the bowling, but she found that her date had greater respect for her. He got her home as requested. Usually, he just said that he would call her sometime. This time, he asked for another date as he was saying good night. Winifred felt a new sense of control over events and over her life. She had taken a major step toward being assertive with men.

Assertiveness and Assertiveness Training

Workshops, lectures, and books on assertiveness are very popular lately. Assertive behavior is not the same as aggressive behavior. To be aggressive is to bring injury to others; to be assertive is merely to try to obtain one's due. In an assertiveness-training program, you are admonished to beware of those who would usurp your position, whether it be on the job or on the line at the grocery store. In order to help people be more assertive gradually, in the small steps required for success, participants are requested to carry out certain homework assignments. For example:

> Ask a question in class (if you are a student).
> Make an announcement (for example, at a P.T.A. meeting).
> Introduce yourself to a stranger in a public place (but watch out).
> Complain to the management.
> Ask someone to save your place on line.
> Second the motion.
> Request change of a twenty-dollar bill without making a purchase.
> Change your mind after the clerk has rung up your order.
> Ask the flight attendant to wire ahead to confirm your connecting flight.

Get the idea? You can probably think up some homework assignments of your own. I am not comfortable about any that involve putting some innocent and overworked clerk to additional trouble, but many of them can be found that really do not involve inconvenience to others.

We can use imagination to help prepare for greater assertiveness. Imagine being on line when someone tries to cut in ahead of you. The nonassertive or ineptly assertive person will become flustered and angry and possibly say nothing out of fear of a scene. Imagine a response that would be polite, firm, and successful. Watching how others handle the situation can be helpful. What happens when someone else is cut in on? You could create the situation by being the person who cuts in.

Lucinda wanted to find a really effective way of dealing with the situation of having someone get ahead of her on line. To discover the strategies and reactions used by others, she deliberately tried to cut into a movie line. Although she is shy in such situations and would never cut in normally, she found that the artificiality of the situation gave her the needed courage and she was able to do it.

She cut in several times in a movie line, being careful that she did not cut in on someone who had seen her cut in on someone else. She pretended confusion, and if no one said anything to her, she left after a moment.

The reactions varied from shouting hostility ("Hey, lady, what do you think you're doing!") to silence accompanied by glares of annoyance. Most effective both in getting her to move away and in maintaining a polite and respectful interaction was the person who tapped her lightly on the shoulder and said, "Pardon me, but I believe you are in the wrong place. You may not realize it but the line begins down there."

That response was most effective because it gave the wrongdoer a face-saving way to leave. Most of those who were aggressive and hostile seemed to assume that Lucinda would not move, and this made it difficult for her to do so without appearing to act simply out of fear of the person who had spoken. Although Lucinda planned to move away after a few minutes no matter what was said, when she was given what sounded like an angry order, she felt herself wanting to stay just to fight back. She could see how this situation generated the kinds of feelings that led to fights.

Romantic Attachments

Romantic love figures prominently in song and fiction, but is virtually ignored within the profound and serious tomes of behavioral sciences. You can look up "love" in books on psychology and psychiatry and not even find "romantic love" there. (What might be there is inability to express love, parental love, love of country, or love of money.) You can look in the many new sexology books; romantic love is not there either. Yet there is no getting away from the fact that for most people, their "love life" is a dominating interest. It is also a factor in long periods of agonized yearning and depression, and in many real-life tragedies, including homicides and suicides.

Mutual love between sexual partners can also be the most intensely pleasurable experience known. The difference between whether it is pain or joy often depends on what one perceives the other person's reaction to be. With evidence that your feelings are returned, you walk on clouds; at any evidence of rejection, you sink to terrible unhappiness. Romantic love is hardly unselfish; in fact, it is very egoistic. And it is a game in which there are winners and losers. The flame may grow intense, but then flicker out readily if a wrong move is made during the crucial period of implantation. Some persons learn the game without ever winning the real prize. Others fall in love with them, but they do not themselves succumb. The prize is mutuality, and you must be vulnerable to be in the running.

You may deplore the fact that skill is necessary for

success in the game of love, but you cannot escape that reality. Only those lucky persons whose skills are so ingrained as to be virtually "unconscious" are blessed with the erroneous feeling that they can be honest with their lover at all times and still win in love.

Lyn met Fred at the library. It seemed to begin casually enough when she dropped her pencil and it rolled across the floor to rest under his chair. It turned out that they left the library at the same time and naturally chatted as they walked along to the subway together. Although they made no appointment to meet again, the next time they happened to meet at the library they went out afterward together to eat.

Lyn never knew that Fred had been observing her for weeks, hoping for the kind of opportunity finally provided by the pencil. After they had been dating for a few months, Lyn found herself in love with Fred and she told him so immediately. In fact, she wondered if they might consider cohabiting. Fred, who had been totally enamored of Lyn at the outset mainly on the basis of physical appearance, had become less ardent as he got to know her better, especially as he discovered the "limitations of her thinking in areas of great importance to him." Had Fred originally been too open about his feelings, he might have scared Lyn away at the outset. Later, by making herself too available and by assuring Fred of the intensity of her feelings for him, Lyn lost ground. Now Fred was the one who was running away.

Unreturned feelings of romantic attachment can be threatening. Persons loved but not loving, or not certain of their feelings, feel smothered by the attentions, promises, and demands of those in love with them. Skillful lovers give no more than what can be comfortably accepted, but when you are in love it is hard to be skillful. The overriding concern of the person in love is fear of being rejected. This fear, and the anxiety and shyness it causes, makes it difficult to do the right thing at the right moment. People with the so-called Don Juan mentality are not in love themselves, so they don't suffer that fear, and thus can be more controlled and can utilize more effective strategies.

The strategy which induces romantic attraction in another and which causes it to endure is difficult when you are in love because it runs precisely counter to your yearnings. You want to be with your lover; effective tactics may require restraint, "playing hard to get." Many feel that using stratagems instead of expressing feelings openly is philosophically unjustifiable. I agree. But, in reality, what evokes the romantic love reaction in another may mean you either play the game or lose. So you are faced with the conflict: Give way to your feelings and maybe scare your lover away or pretend to care less than you do in order to enhance your appeal. Philosophical values may have to be put aside for a while since true expression of feelings early in the game may bring defeat.

It is not simply a matter of being hard to get, for attraction depends on giving some indication of interest. The effective lover offers hope, not certainty, which is a very difficult task for the person who has in fact already fallen in love.

Carla was so afraid of coming on too strong and frightening Tom off that she erred in the opposite direction. Wanting desperately to go to the coffee machine when she noted that he was there taking a break, she feared looking obvious, so she stayed at her desk. In fact, Tom had no idea that she was at all interested in him.

To self-manage your love life probably requires more skills and planning than any other aspect of your social behavior.

The most difficult problem to be dealt with is how to keep yourself from suffering when your lover has rejected you. When you are brokenhearted, often your work does not get done and you spend your days in misery. Inability to function can occur at all capability levels, increasing a person's temptation to find relief in alcohol or other drugs. Jealousy can lead to intensification of the painful feelings. Or there may be dull but persistent depression accompanied by disinclination to remain in the company of others. To get relief, block off the thoughts that bring the image of ecstasy. These are the ones that cause the feelings to persist. Find the locus of body sensation and concentrate your attention on the sensation itself. Meditate on it until discomfort slowly subsides. Simple attempts at distraction, on the other hand, can do more harm than good. One can still be obsessed over one's lost love while watching a movie or flying in a plane. Learn to substitute other thoughts and to ease out that pain-inducing image of the rapturous embrace that seems, when love is at its height, to be the one desired goal above all others.

Managing Your Sex Life

Just as we are not always the same when it comes to our ability to perform complex intellectual tasks, we are not always the same when it comes to our sexual appetites, inclinations, and ability to function (or "perform"). Sometimes our partner is not up to it. Sometimes we ourselves are the ones not interested. "Performance" problems are somewhat related to problems of being busy, having different schedules, and sometimes simply the difficulty of finding time for sex. In spite of all the obstacles, when we have the opportunity for sex, we hate to waste it.

Harry was the one who suggested that he and Stella do a Sex Readiness Levels Analysis. Just as when analyzing capability levels, they recorded their degree of sexual interest on a five-point scale from One (meaning very interested) to Five (meaning not at all interested). They discovered that in five years of married life they had never had sex at the time that both of their sex readiness levels were highest. And no wonder. To their great surprise, for them most intense sexual interest potential occurred in the morning.

There are also the problems of finding suitable sexual partners and of your extrasexual relationship with them. Most people accept the notion that sex without love—or at least sex without a good, respectful friendship—is undesirable, even perverse. Members of both sexes complain if they feel they are "wanted only for my body." Because we have "relationships" with sex partners, or feel we ought to, it can be hard to be efficient when it comes to sex.

Virginia liked sex. It lifted her spirits and it relaxed her. But she had no time for dinners and dancing and shows and long conversations. She dreamed of being able to have a "sex break" midmorning at the office or finding a lover who would come to her home at nine in the evening and be willing to leave at eleven after a two-hour session that would leave her in a perfect mood for contented sleep. Instead, she found that her lovers wanted to "take her out," spend long hours in conversation, and make love until dawn. Consequently, she spent much less time having sex than she would have liked.

Once, with a man she liked very much, with whom sex was especially satisfying, and with whom there had been a long-standing relationship that seemed good and trusting but not overly intense, she tried to restructure the situation. She cautiously suggested that they try to see each other more often but for shorter periods of time, that sometimes they have purely sex dates which would not cause too much interference with sleep and with their busy schedules, yet allow for more sex. The man was outraged. He stormed out of her apartment and out of her life. She did not dare to bring up the matter with anyone else for a long time after that.

Sometimes marriage is the perfect solution to this problem but even your marriage partner may resent the suggestion that sex take place any other way than "romantically."

Too often, sex occurs after a long evening after a long day, when both partners are not only exhausted, but also feeling the effects of a few drinks. Less propitious conditions can hardly be imagined.

Sue and Mike were on the verge of ending their relationship altogether. It seemed clear that they were sexually incompatible, although in the earlier stages of their relationship sex had been very good indeed. Now they had gotten into the habit of going to a midweek movie together, and of visiting friends or going dancing with other couples on Saturday night. Sex occurred afterward. Sometimes Mike was unable to get an erection; sometimes Sue said she was very tired. Rarely, they managed to have the kind of session that they used to have.

One evening, when Mike arrived at seven o'clock in the evening to pick Sue up for a movie, he found her in a dressing gown. She took his hand and led him to the bedroom. "Mike," she said, "I want you and I want you now. If we miss the movie, we can watch TV. Let's go to bed first."

That change in the order of events was so successful that it became standard for them.

Maybe the reason it is customary to leave sex for the end of the evening hearkens back to the days when it was considered shameful to have it at all. Or maybe it has something to do with not wanting to mess up a bed before bedtime. If that's it, you might want to reevaluate your priorities!

There is also the matter of privacy. In most homes, privacy is easier to come by when the rest of the family is sleeping.

Dora's children were both in elementary school. They spent the early evening doing homework, then usually watched television until bedtime at nine or nine-thirty. On Friday and Saturday evening, they sometimes stayed up until ten-thirty or eleven. It was only in the middle of the night, after midnight, that Dora and her husband felt that they were assured of sufficient privacy to engage in sexual relations.

The need for privacy should never be underestimated. Lack of assurance that one's lovemaking session will not be intruded on can be very important. Fear of intrusion is distracting, and distraction is a major cause of performance disappointments. How does one achieve privacy? Planning, firmness, and a lock on the door!

Sometimes one partner is distracted and the other is not, or their times of distraction do not coincide.

Vera had had a grueling weekend attending a conference at which she had had to make a speech. For two days, she had endured intense social interactions, including some heated arguments. It was a real relief to get home Sunday evening to find her lover, Marc, waiting for her. For one thing, she was able to let off some steam by telling about the weekend's event to a sympathetic ear. After a couple of hours of talk and a drink or two, they went to bed. Vera was tired, but feeling very affectionate and grateful.

Marc liked sex, and he liked a sexual session to include more than one orgasm. The first was just a warm-up. But this night, after the first, he found himself the victim of a condition he rarely experienced, but often feared: he could not get an erection. Probably something about the evening—maybe Vera's exuberance about things in which he had played no role—was distracting him. After a while, Vera, who was really fatigued, fell asleep.

And, after a longer while, Marc, lying beside her, found that his organ had returned to functional condition; his penis was erect and he was ready for more action. But the previously willing Vera was now inert. She responded to his attempts to arouse her by saying, very sleepily, that she was too tired, and she stretched across the bed in a way that made it clear she wanted Marc to leave her alone.

Two days later, when Marc called about something related to their mutual business interests, Vera cheerfully wondered when they would be able to get together again. She was shocked to find that Marc was angry at her. Vera apologized and Marc warmed up a bit. He apologized, too. "I'm sorry," he said, "I knew you were tired. But it was so frustrating first to be unable to do it and then to have you reject me when I finally could."

Human relationships are delicate. Interpersonal sex exists within those relationships. If a good relationship is to be sustained, it may require some self-management. Sometimes simply recognizing the other person's situation can take you a long way.

Being a Person

This book has not dealt with such projects as increasing your femininity, your physical attractiveness, or your cooking ability, although if you select these as goals, the self-management principles can help you attain them. Repeatedly, I have emphasized that in self-management *you* choose the goals.

We are in a period of cultural change concerning what behaviors are deemed appropriate for women, and, generally, the direction is toward "androgyny," that is, toward decreased differentiation of what is considered appropriate behavior by females and by males. The more androgynous you are, the less "feminine" or "masculine" you are whatever your sex. The fact that many women and men born, reared, and conditioned in a society that accepted traditional sex roles have already made changes in their personal life-styles in the direction of androgynous (and feminist) values, is testimony to human adaptability. The aim of this book is to help you achieve a life-style that will bring you greater happiness. Perhaps its most basic assumption is that you can change in the direction of whatever goals you select for yourself.

But of course that is not the whole story. Others constrain us through their expectations. That women are discriminated against has only recently been extensively recognized. What we now view as sexist was formerly thought normal and natural. Now we understand that the portrayal of women in fiction and in textbooks as weak and dependent on males is not a "true reflection of reality," but a method of hiding and denying female potential.

In our time of social change we can make more use of our capacities. That there have been no female Einsteins, Bachs, or Newtons is not evidence of our inferiority but of the suppression of female talent. There is no scientific evidence of female inferiority. Most behavioral differences between the sexes are culturally determined. Little girls today are thinking of themselves as potential baseball players, scientists, and political leaders. But sexism is still very much with us, and one of our problems is how to deal with it.

The most common way you might handle sexism is to pretend it isn't there. If you look around, you can see that most of us are accustomed to being treated in ways that a feminist would find insulting. We usually do not speak up; often we are not aware of what is happening. To some degree, we save ourselves grief by burying our heads in the sand. It's bad enough to be paid less for equal or superior work; it hurts more to realize that it is happening. But it gets harder and harder to deny the evidence of prejudice against us and to ignore problems that result solely from our being the object of sexism.

What should we do when faced directly with sexist and insulting behavior? What should we say to the person who assumes that what we say is unimportant, or that we could not possibly know anything about how a car works, or that we are too emotional to be able to deal with emergencies or to handle serious responsibilities? When we are not even considered for a managerial position, these attitudes may be behind the discrimination. Whether they are expressed in the form of a joke, a bit of homespun philosophy, or an indictment of you personally, they severely limit your freedom to fulfill yourself by finding your most appropriate role. Even the ability to function in the woman's universally-accepted roles is hindered by sexism—for example, when a mother is not taken as seriously as her husband would be when she describes her child's symptoms to the pediatrician; or, if alone, when she is unable to support herself and her children the way she could if she were male.

And what about those social occasions in which someone—usually a man, but sometimes a woman—tells a joke in which the humor depends on the stereotyped pictures of female ineptness, emotionality, seductiveness, or plain stupidity? What do we do? Do we fight back and convert a pleasant situation into an argument? Wouldn't we risk both social censure and the draining of our emotional energy? The problem arises more and more once the process of so-called "conciousness-raising" has begun, a process in which we see old things in new ways. Sometimes our self-respect will demand that we speak up. At other times, we may elect to avoid future interaction with the offending individuals.

But what if the culprit is a husband or your own child? Then the problem is especially serious. Utilizing the self-management principles can be very important in dealing with it. The first step, of course, involves observation and analysis of the actual initial situation and the setting of goals.

It wasn't that Charles was basically a male chauvinist; it was more that he had found a topic of conversation that unfailingly elicited a response from others. Elise, his wife, however, was both embarrassed and angered by his poking fun at "libbers" and antiwomen joking.

For two weeks, she counted instances. There were twelve of them, ranging from a "joke" about dumb blond secretaries to an observation on "fat women in pants." When the incidents occurred, Elise tried her best to keep her reactions what they always had been—sometimes seething silently, other times expressing her distaste for his behavior. She also noticed instances of a positive attitude toward women. These were harder to find, but there were actually four such occasions.

After the baseline interval, she began using positive reinforcement when her husband's conversation was not offensive. This took several forms: asking if he wanted something to eat or drink, giving "spontaneous" kisses or hugs, or bringing up one of his favorite topics. When the offending remarks occurred, she said nothing. If possible, she quietly left the room for a few minutes.

It took time, but her strategies worked. After two months, Charles was no longer making male chauvinist jokes and comments. In fact, he had begun to understand the feminist viewpoint.

Elise was helped by others who were also tired of Charles's antifeminist talk and had stopped giving him

the positive attention such behavior had formerly com-
manded. The situation is more difficult to handle when
the offending individual is receiving support for his
sexist behavior from peers.

Geraldine tried with her ten-year-old son, Jamey, the same methods that Elise used but progress was very slow. It seemed that such
talk was the current fashion with the gang of kids he hung around
with. But she did not give up, and eventually Jamey began to
improve. Geraldine was not sure that his behavior had changed
when he was not in her presence, but at least she no longer had
to listen to it.

Women have also become concerned about street
harassment. Some have concluded that the time-
honored reaction to men in the street who make unwel-
come complimentary comments about their physical
appearance or obscene remarks—that of pretending not
to notice—is not effective in reducing the occurrence of
such events. Some have begun to react emphatically by
speaking back, sometimes in kind. But this may escalate
the situation. Here is a situation that shows how forth-
right action can produce an effective solution.

Harriet and Trudy were harassed by construction workers as they
passed the site on their way to the office where both were employed as social workers. The two women immediately took the
matter to the men's employer.

These men's behavior is in fact punishable by the same
laws that permit the police to arrest prostitutes who "ha-
rass respectable businessmen."

Changing the behavior of others is one part of the
problem. Another is dealing with one's own emotional
reaction.

Ginny was hit slightly by the car behind her. The driver, annoyed with himself and her, got out and began to lambaste her, blaming "women drivers" in general and Ginny in particular for stopping her car abruptly. Ginny decided not to react at all. She sat in her car calmly and relaxed while he raved. By keeping cool she prevented escalation and still gave him no satisfaction.

Whether action or inaction is called for may depend on the particular set of circumstances. Generally, you are probably wisest to develop a self-management program designed to change the behavior of those who are close to you while looking for assistance from others, including the law, when you deal with strangers.

The problem is especially difficult when the offending individual is a person in authority.

Verne's boss thought it was very witty to continuously make comments about the physical attractiveness of his office workers. He was insensitive to the women's growing resentment. Verne decided to do something about the daily insults to which the women felt they were being subjected. She organized a luncheon meeting to discuss the issue. The women decided to write a letter to the boss with all their signatures on it, telling him politely but firmly how they felt. They were very careful to describe the offending behaviors so that there could be no question in his mind as to what they were referring.

Next morning, chagrined, their boss apologized. Furthermore, his behavior changed.

Harassment is only one very small part of a woman's problem with sexism. Discrimination is a much larger part. It is difficult for victims of discrimination ever to be certain that prejudice against them on the basis of sex is really the problem rather than some individual failing. Before the recent feminist activism, a woman literally had nowhere to turn. Now, there are government and feminist organizations that can help. Sex discrimination is just as illegal as discrimination on the basis of race or religion. It does exist, and a woman who understands that it does is better prepared to react with assertion and dignity when a problem comes up. Formerly, women and others discriminated against were accused of being "thin-skinned" or "paranoid" if they complained. That was part of the discrimination pattern. But when a job or promotion or raise in pay is not granted, it is very important to understand why. It is important to your psychological well-being that you not blame yourself when it is in fact sexism that underlies your ill-fortune.

Ruth was a college instructor in physics. She was passed over for promotion with the excuse that her students did not find her stimulating. She was very upset and vowed to improve. She developed new teaching strategies, but these also failed. The problem was that the students were prejudiced against a woman scientist. There was no way that she could deal with the problem through changing her teaching skills, which were in fact excellent.

Knocking one's head against a stone wall can do no more than ruin a good head. Recognizing when failure is inevitable is also a part of effective self-management.

With self-management you can dictate your own actions freed from habits that kept you from doing what you wanted to have done. You can develop your potential in your current field, or maybe strike out in some new direction, you can develop a skill you always wanted but never found time for, you can improve your social, sex, and love relationships, you can organize your work and your time so that life is more pleasant on a day-to-day basis, you can improve your attractiveness and your physical health, and you can generally enjoy your life more because you are taking steps towards the attainment of your longer-range goals and because you are coddling yourself on the way. Now, it's up to you to examine your present situation, decide where you want to go, and take the first small step.

It's the time to begin the creation of your new, self-managed Super Self!

Appendix: A Brief Summary of Strategies, Principles, Tactics, and Homely Adages

Some of the principles of self-management which have been presented in this book have been scientifically studied and can also be found in the textbooks on self-management, a new psychology field. Here they have sometimes been stripped of their technical terminology, but you will probably have little difficulty recognizing them when you meet them under other names.

Other principles are more obvious and common-sensical. All have met at least the test of usage by me, my students, my colleagues, and my clients. I restate them now as a quick and convenient guide:

The Principle of Planning. Virtually all the stratagems and tactics of self-management require that we first observe and analyze rather than jump in feet first. If we did the latter, we might possibly fail because of factors not considered or events that were unanticipated. We do not simply resolve to change; we plan precisely how the changes will be brought about.

Failure Is a Failure of a Program, Not of You. This general principle means that when things do not work out as planned, we reevaluate the program and make changes. We do not feel guilty or angry with ourselves; we "go back to the drawing board" to devise a more efficient plan.

The Principle of Small Steps. In various forms and under various names, this principle has been supported again and again by the research in psychology and education. If a task is too difficult, break it down. If you try to take too large a step you may fail to reach a goal that is easily attainable taken small step by small step. Other expressions convey the same or a similar idea. For example, the principle of *shaping (or successive approximations)* refers to beginning with a very small step in the desired direction, so that you can develop new behaviors or reach interim goals toward your ultimate goal. The principles of *warm-up* and of *finding an entrance* state that even with a familiar activity, some small steps may help get it going.

The Principle of Antecedents. This principle tells us that cues in the environment may call forth certain behaviors if those cues have been previously associated with them. Being aware of this principle, you might sit at your desk to get in the mood for studying or paying bills, or place a sign on the kitchen counter saying "Don't Eat Too Much!" The principle of *arranging the environment* basically has to do with the same idea. Children will not put their toys away if there is no place to put them. People are more inclined to engage in conversation if their chairs are placed so that they are within earshot of one another. You are following the same principle when you turn your ring around your finger in a manner that you are not used to wearing it to remind you to make a phone call, or when you place an egg-timer by the telephone to help you shorten long-distance calls, or put your key ring over the ignition key to prevent you from leaving your auto lights on all day after using them in the morning fog. We react to our environment, but we can also make changes in it that guide our behavior.

Many unwanted actions are elicited by environmental cues. A bowl full of crisp, crunchy potato chips calls forth eating. So what do you do if you want to limit eating? Remove the temptation. The *substitute list* to which you refer when you get an urge to give in to a consummatory behavior you are trying to reduce or eliminate is a cue you have placed in your environment so that you will be more likely to resort to alternatives to the unwanted behavior. It's another form of managing yourself through your environment.

The Principle of Reinforcement.   This is one of the best researched principles ever to come out of a psychology lab. It works with worms, rats, monkeys, children, men, and us. Actions followed by pleasing events are strengthened thereby. When we talk of *consequents,* we are giving careful consideration to what results our behavior will have. In a self-management program we follow the hard task with the easier one, and the harder one becomes easier. In managing the behavior of others, *look for the good,* knowing your attention and praise will strengthen the desirable behaviors that you find.

The opposite of reinforcement is not punishment but the principle that *when an action produces no result, it will be discontinued.* In psychological jargon, this is called "extinction." A mother discovers that her attention is inadvertently reinforcing her toddler's temper outbursts. When she changes tactics and ignores the tantrums, they may increase in severity at first but will eventually go away.

We do not use punishment. It may "work" sometimes, but it may make you want to give up altogether and forget the whole business. Reinforce yourself when you improve; do not punish yourself if you don't. Reevaluate.

Getting rid of undesirable behaviors is best accomplished by means of the principle of *strengthening incompatible alternatives.* To reduce fidgeting, increase sitting still. To reduce drinking alcoholic beverages, drink water or soda. This is the same as our principle of *finding substitutes.*

Capability and Activity Levels Analyses.   These methods will not be found elsewhere in just this form, but research findings on "biorhythms" and circadian fluctuations and periodicities are consistent with them. Use your knowledge of when your various levels are likely to occur during the day to schedule your activities. By being sensitive to levels, you will function more efficiently. Awareness that *life is lived at all levels* will help keep you from feeling bad when you find yourself at a lower level than you would like. By using the principle of *not shifting too far downward,* you will be encouraged to make the best use of your capability level at any given moment.

Some of the other principles discussed in the book are scientifically based; others are straight out of Aunt Harriet's Helpful Hints. Here are a few more:

> Make friendly assumptions
> Recognize the law of giving and taking
> Be aware that whenever you are angry at someone, you are probably more angry at yourself
> Appreciate "luck" and that "every cloud has a silver lining"
> Watch others (the principle of modeling)

Discover Your Own Rules

These principles have proven their value to others and I'm sure they will do so for you, but they are not the only useful self-management principles. Many more undoubtedly await discovery. As you develop your own self-management programs, you'll surely add your own rules, hints, and techniques. Look for them. Coddling means adopting whatever strategy is effective for a given task. It means that if you have a problem, you find a solution—a realistic one, one that you can live with.

A French book teaches French. A math book teaches math. Self-management gets you to study.

A diet book gives instructions on how to lose weight. Self-management gets you to stick to the diet.

Drag out all those self-improvement books you gave up on in disgust. Get them down from the attic or up from the basement. Self-management helps you to put their wisdom into action.

Index

About the Author

Dorothy Tennov, Ph.D., an experimental and behaviorist psychologist, is Professor of Psychology at the University of Bridgeport, and has a private behavioral consultation practice in Stratford, Connecticut.

Super Self is her second book. The first, *Psychotherapy: The Hazardous Cure* (Abelard-Schuman, 1975) is a critical examination and analysis of the tactics of psychiatrists, psychologists, social workers, and others who conduct individual talking therapy and the effects of their methods on those who present themselves for psychotherapy treatment. *Super Self* is part of the answer to the question of alternatives to the expense and the hazards of trying to get help from psychotherapy.

Dr. Tennov is also working on a textbook and training manual on the management of the behavior of children, and she is conducting scientific research related to capability levels and to romantic attachments. The latter is expected to be the topic of her next book for the general public.